MW01044543

People

YEARBOOK
2011

124

60

48

56

68

4

64

112

News & Events

AT THE NEXUS OF POP CULTURE, ROMANCE AND CELEBRITY, NO STORY WAS
BIGGER THAN SANDRA BULLOCK'S CLASSY COPING WITH A DRAMATIC YEAR

HEARTBREAK AND JOY

Remarkable and Resilient

Sandra BULLOCK

You could say Sandra Bullock had an eventful year, but that's like saying Facebook has a few members. Coming off a spectacular 2009, in which her cutesy rom-com *The Proposal* and her football-themed weepie *The Blind Side* were both surprise blockbusters, Bullock became—at age 46— Hollywood's most bankable female star not named Meryl Streep. Then the career capper: this year's Best Actress Oscar for playing a tough Memphis socialite in *Blind Side*. "Did I really earn this, or did I just wear you all down?" she asked in her acceptance speech, with hubby Jesse James beaming in the front row.

But just days after her Oscar triumph, Bullock herself got blindsided: Reports surfaced that James had cheated

AND THE
WINNER IS...

Bullock's big
post-Oscar goal?
"I want to be able
to enjoy being
a mom," said the
actress (in L.A.
in May '09).

on her with several women. "I had no idea about anything," she later told PEOPLE. "Never in a million years did I foresee something like this happening." Bullock filed for divorce in April, and soon the couple's five-year marriage was over.

But all that was mere warm-up for the real bombshell. In May, Bullock turned up on the cover of PEOPLE kissing adorable Louis Bardo Bullock, a baby she adopted from New Orleans and raised secretly since January. "I don't know how we got away with it," she said of dodging paparazzi during the busiest time of her career, surely as impressive a feat as winning an Oscar. Bullock, who had no children but was helping raise James' three kids, actually began searching for a baby with James four years ago. "There were so many children alone after Katrina, and for some reason we knew that someone would want to come into our lives," she said. But when she finally got the call about a possible place-ment earlier this year, "I panicked," said Bullock. "It came right in the middle of all the media craziness of awards season. I just didn't understand why the universe was deciding a child needed to be with us now. Of all times!" Then she laid eyes on Louis for the first time, and "the whole outside world just got quiet. It was like he had always been a part of our lives."

After her split with James, Bullock finalized the adoption as a single mother (she has not discussed the details of the adoption or James' role in raising Louis). Named after jazz great Louis Armstrong—"'What a Wonderful World' kept playing in my head when I looked at him"—the tyke has turned her into one of those moms who can't stop yapping about her kid. "I'm telling everyone I meet about the most beautiful man I know," she said, "including his poop schedule!" She could write her own ticket in Hollywood now—*The Proposal* and *The Blind Side* earned nearly half a billion bucks combined—but "the career will have to wait for a bit." Instead, she'll focus on feedings, burpings and bibs. "To say that I am changed is an understatement," said Bullock. "I never imagined I would say the words 'my son.'"

JESSE JAMES MOVES ON

The bad boy biker-reality TV star tried saving his marriage by entering rehab in March. "Sandy is the love of my life," he said. After the divorce, James dated tattoo artist Kat Von D, 28.

A YEAR IN THE LIFE OF SANDRA…

LET THE AWARDS SEASON BEGIN! The day before the Oscars—and displaying exceptional sportsmanship—Bullock accepted a Worst Actress razzie for her role in *All About Steve*.

GRATEFUL WINNER Bullock tearfully thanked her mother, Helga, an opera singer who died in 2000.

MERYLLY, MERYLLY She smooched Streep at an awards show in January, saying, Meryl's "a good kisser!"

NEW ORLEANS Bullock (in August) opened a health clinic she helped fund.

THE BRIGHT SIDE With her son Louis in July. "As long as he knows he is loved," she said, "then I will have done my job as a mama."

OSCAR NIGHT Bullock and James were all smiles after her big win in March. Just days later they split up.

NIGHTMARE
IN THE GULF

t happened in the dark of night, in the middle of nowhere—an explosion on a drilling rig 41 miles off the coast of Louisiana. That April 20 blast aboard the *Deepwater Horizon*, caused by a buildup of methane gas, killed 11 workers and triggered the worst oil spill in U.S. history. With British Petroleum unable to stop the flow—and bumbling BP CEO Tony Heyward griping, "I'd like my life back"—some 5 million barrels of crude oil spewed from the well in three months, crippling the Gulf of Mexico's commercial fishing industry and threatening wetlands. "I lost everything in Hurricane Katrina, but this is worse," said Louisiana fisherman Al Cassagne.

BP finally capped the well on July 15, but by then gobs of crude had washed up on beaches and the giant oil slick was visible from space. Massive cleanup efforts, likely to cost billions, continue. "We're strong and we can get past this," said Cassagne. "We'll never give up."

A rescuer helps a sludge-covered pelican.

The burning oil
rig on April 21.

"I FELT EMBARRASSED FOR HAVING BEEN SO DECEIVED. I FELT BETRAYED"

"I thought only about myself," Woods said at his Feb. 19 press conference. "I am deeply sorry."

ELIN'S STORY

t was the crash heard round the world—Tiger Woods driving into a fire hydrant late one night in November 2009. That kicked off a sex scandal that stalled his career as the planet's best golfer and doomed his almost six-year marriage to Elin Nordegren, mother of their two children, Sam, 3, and Charlie, 1. While Woods, 35, spent the year awkwardly apologizing for his many affairs—"I lied to myself," he said at one press conference—Nordegren, 30, kept silent and out of sight. Finally, after they divorced in August, she told her story to PEOPLE. "The word betrayal isn't strong enough," she said of learning of Woods' indiscretions. "I felt like my whole world had fallen apart."

She and Woods "tried really hard" to save their marriage, Nordegren said. Yet it was not to be. The divorce is estimated to have netted her more than $100 million, but "money can't buy happiness or put my family back together," she said. Instead she focused on getting her degree in psychology and settling into new digs in Florida, where Woods—whose return to golf has been rocky—has "shared parental responsibility" for the children. And while she won't rule out dating, "it's going to be just me and the kids for a little while," said Nordegren. "But I believe in love because I've seen it. I've been there."

BAD DAY AT WORK

Some fans booed Woods not long after his return to golf at the Quail Hollow Championship in Charlotte, N.C.

Earthquake in Haiti

A SHATTERING
ACT OF GOD

There was no ominous thundercloud, no wailing siren. One minute the ground was still. The next, at 4:53 p.m. on Jan. 12, something terrible had begun. A 7.0 earthquake shook Port-au-Prince, the capital of Haiti, and the surrounding area—the most devastating earthquake to hit the poor Caribbean nation in centuries. Shoddy construction standards led to unthinkable levels of damage; the Haitian government estimated more than 230,000 people were killed, with another 2 million left homeless.

The catastrophe is an enduring one: Hundreds of thousands of people still have no homes, and untold billions will be needed to rebuild what was lost. As the earthquake happened, "the floor underneath my desk was opening, like it was trying to suck me down," said bank loan officer Fabienne Leger. "Everybody was running for their lives." Factory worker Benitot Revolus spent four days trapped beneath rubble before being rescued. "There in the dark I said, 'Lord, I'm so young, is there really a need to take me now?'" he recalled. Money, supplies and medical care poured in from around the world—George Clooney's Hope for Haiti telethon in January raised nearly $60 million—but a year later, Haiti is still reeling. "Life is hard, very hard," said survivor Marcus Francois, 19. "But we are strong."

The earthquake leveled Haiti's presidential palace in Port-au-Prince.

Medics help an injured child. As many as 3 million people were at risk of infection.

A CITY
IN RUINS

A survivor
walks through
the rubble. By
some estimates,
half of Port-
au-Prince's
buildings were
damaged or
destroyed.

THE REALITY TV TANGO

Bristol "had this fantasy for Tripp: Mom and Dad at home," says her aunt Molly McCann. "Now she's heartbroken." A few months later she did the cha-cha on *Dancing with the Stars* with partner Mark Ballas.

FADING LEVI

ON JULY 14, Bristol Palin and her baby's daddy, Levi Johnston, announced their reengagement in the press—which is also how her mother, Sarah Palin, got the news. "We obviously want what's best for our children," Bristol's parents said in a statement notably devoid of pre-wedding excitement. "Bristol believes in redemption and forgiveness to a degree most of us struggle to put in practice."

Three weeks later, Bristol, 19, dumped Johnston, 20, after discovering he'd made a music video that mocked her family. Moving back to her parents' house (there were "no I-told-you-so's," said Palin) with son Tripp, then 18 months, she was soon prepping in L.A. for her debut on *Dancing with the Stars*.

THE EX FILES

In August, Johnston declared his candidacy for mayor of Wasilla, Alaska.

Johnston posed for *Playgirl*'s Winter 2010 cover. "He's just obsessed with the limelight, and I got played," said Bristol.

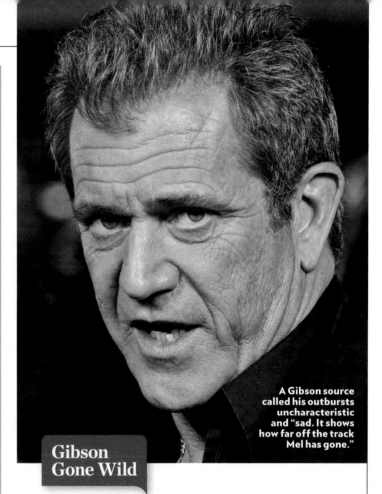

A Gibson source called his outbursts uncharacteristic and "sad. It shows how far off the track Mel has gone."

Gibson Gone Wild

RANTING SUPERSTAR?

"Threaten you?" the familiar voice says in spitting exasperation. "I'll put you in a [expletive] rose garden, you [expletive]! You understand that?" There's more, including "You need a [expletive] bat in the side [of] the head. All right, how about that?" The tapes, made by Oksana Grigorieva, allegedly of her estranged lover Mel Gibson, appeared on Radaronline.com and turned what had been a difficult split into an end-of-days conflagration. Grigorieva, 40, claimed an enraged Gibson had also hit her more than once; Gibson, 54, denied that charge and said his ex had been using their child Lucia, 1, as a pawn to extort money from him. Various investigations are trying to determine who did what, and what's best for Lucia. Of Gibson, a friend says, "He loves that baby. He's okay as long as he's with her."

"He gets angry for no specific reason," says Grigorieva (with Gibson in February '10).

LINDSEY
VONN

Days before the
Olympics, Vonn, 26,
disclosed she had
an "excruciatingly
painful" shin injury.
But bad weather
on the slopes
postponed races
long enough for the
two-time World Cup
overall champion
to mend and grab
the women's
downhill gold by
0.56 of a second in a
spectacular run.

APOLO ANTON OHNO

Short-track skating star Ohno, 28, has won more career medals (eight) than any other U.S. Winter Olympian, thanks to a silver and two bronzes in Vancouver.

O Canada!

OLYMPIC HUSTLE

AT FIRST THE 2010 Winter Olympics in Vancouver appeared headed for calamity: A Georgian luger died in a practice run before the games opened, freakily warm weather turned slopes to slush, and the Olympic cauldron's hydraulic system malfunctioned during the opening ceremonies. But then competition began, and when the snowflakes settled, Americans had set a new record for the most medals won by a single country (37). Some memorable moments: Lindsey Vonn becoming the first American woman to win the downhill; Evan Lysacek upsetting Russia's heavily favored Evgeni Plushenko in men's figure skating; and the first-ever American gold in the oft-overlooked Nordic Combined—a combo of ski jumping and cross-country racing—won by Billy Demong, who was selected to carry the American flag during the closing ceremonies.

SHAUN WHITE

White, 24, already had enough points for the gold, "but I came all the way to Vancouver to do something amazing," he said. So, for an encore, he threw a Double McTwist 1260—two flips plus 3½ turns—the most difficult and dangerous half-pipe trick ever attempted.

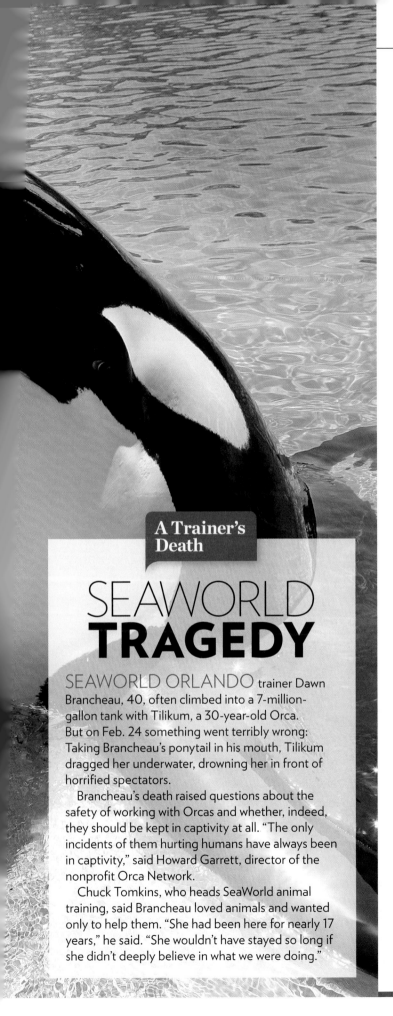

BIG
DEBATE

MOVIE DIRECTOR Kevin Smith, 40, says he knows how people feel about sitting next to the fat guy on the plane; sometimes he'll buy two tickets, he says, "because it's way more comfortable and I have the money." That wasn't the case, though, when he got a standby ticket on a Feb. 13 Southwest Airlines flight and was removed from the plane as a danger to himself and others. "What, was I gonna roll on a fellow passenger?" he tweeted to his million-plus followers. Southwest said he did not fit safely into a single seat and couldn't lower his armrests. Smith says that wasn't true: "I know I'm fat, but I'm not that fat!" His complaints made national news and sparked debate about passenger rights.

A Trainer's Death

SEAWORLD
TRAGEDY

SEAWORLD ORLANDO trainer Dawn Brancheau, 40, often climbed into a 7-million-gallon tank with Tilikum, a 30-year-old Orca. But on Feb. 24 something went terribly wrong: Taking Brancheau's ponytail in his mouth, Tilikum dragged her underwater, drowning her in front of horrified spectators.

Brancheau's death raised questions about the safety of working with Orcas and whether, indeed, they should be kept in captivity at all. "The only incidents of them hurting humans have always been in captivity," said Howard Garrett, director of the nonprofit Orca Network.

Chuck Tomkins, who heads SeaWorld animal training, said Brancheau loved animals and wanted only to help them. "She had been here for nearly 17 years," he said. "She wouldn't have stayed so long if she didn't deeply believe in what we were doing."

"Hey, Southwest, look how fat I am on your plane!" Smith tweeted from a later flight, for which he bought two tickets.

Zinger
Slingers

Singer Alex
Ray Joel

FIGHTING
BACK

I DIDN'T want to get dressed," recalled Alexa Ray Joel of the morning of Dec. 5, 2009. "I didn't want to put on makeup. I hit rock bottom." She took some homeopathic pills. Soon she was sweaty and shaking. Joel dialed 911 and was rushed to a hospital.

The next day, the press reported that the daughter of Billy Joel and Christie Brinkley had tried to take her own life. "I did say 'I want to die' on the [911 call]," Alexa, 25, said later. "Did I really want to? Absolutely not! I was being dramatic, and I . . . apologize to everybody involved."

Her tailspin stemmed, she said, from heartbreak—and the fact that "when you're that depressed, you don't feel anybody is going to understand." With therapy, she says, she found a way past the darkness—and hopes others can too. Said Joel: "I want young men and women to feel they're not alone in depression."

LATE NIGHT
CAT FIGHT

As a strategy, it will no doubt be studied at Harvard business School—for all the wrong reasons: Take the top-rated late night show; dump the host; hand the job over to a hipper guy who appeals to a narrower audience; panic when it doesn't work out; and offend both hosts and their fans while awkwardly trying to give the first guy his old job back. In the end, Conan O'Brien, who quit *The Tonight Show* rather than accept NBC's demand that he start later, delivered the best lines ("I just want to say to the kids out there: You can do anything you want in life—unless Jay Leno wants to do it, too" and "It's hard to accept that I won't have a show, but Snooki and the Situation will"), but it was Leno who, upon his return to Johnny Carson's old chair, made *Tonight* No. 1 again in its time slot. "Coco" O'Brien, meanwhile, prepared to debut his new show on TBS. "I've gone from network television to Twitter to performing live in theaters, and now I'm headed for basic cable," he joked. "My plan is working perfectly!"

NBC FAMILY FEUD

Like so many relationships, O'Brien and Leno's (above, in '03) started great but ended in tears and recriminations. "Hey, NBC said they wanted drama at 10:00," said Leno. "Now they've got it."

"I was in such a dark place," said Joel. "Now . . . everything is new."

"She'd go to great lengths to make someone else happy," a friend said of Prince.

Bullied to Death?

PHOEBE PRINCE

AT HER HIGH SCHOOL in Massachusetts, she was the target of constant taunts—whore, bitch, Irish slut—but Phoebe Prince tried hard not to let it get to her. Her strategy, she told a friend, was to "keep her head high, smile and just let it go." Until she couldn't any longer: On Jan. 14 the pretty 15-year-old from County Clare, Ireland, was found hanging from a noose she had made out of a scarf in her family's home.

Her death, dubbed a "bullycide" by the media, focused a national spotlight on the problem of school bullying. Investigators learned that Phoebe had been shoved into a locker and told on Facebook, "Go kill yourself"; on the day Phoebe took her life, she'd been relentlessly goaded and had had a can thrown at her. "She was beautiful, and she was bullied out of pure jealousy," said one classmate. "She wasn't a tough girl, and she would tell me how scared she was," said a friend. In the end six classmates were charged (see sidebar). Phoebe's death was "horrible, but it's the only reason why these people at school are finally listening," said one parent. "There are just so many Phoebes."

DEADLY BULLIES?

Six of Phoebe's classmates were charged; their trials start in 2011

SEAN MULVEYHILL, 17
A star football player, now charged with statutory rape. One neighbor said, "He comes from a family that really cares about their children."

SHARON CHANON VELAZQUEZ, 16
Suspended after a verbal exchange with Prince. Still, "my daughter never fought with [Prince]," insisted Velazquez' mom.

KAYLA NAREY, 17
A top field-hockey player, she's charged with "violation of civil rights, with bodily injury resulting," a felony. Like all the defendants, she pleaded not guilty.

AUSTIN RENAUD, 18
Prince's relationship with him apparently led to the taunting; he has been charged, as an adult, with statutory rape. "He's a quiet, respectful kid," said his lawyer.

FLANNERY MULLINS, 16
Students told police she threatened to beat Prince up; court records show she posted several harsh Facebook comments directed at Prince.

ASHLEY LONGE, 16
Charges against her include civil rights violation with bodily injury resulting. "She is nervous about the charges and wishes [it] never happened," said a source.

Possessed of a quick mind but not a lot of self-restraint, Mayer rambled about his bedroom habits and used the N-word, for which he later apologized.

JOHN MAYER'S FREE SPEECH

He has won seven Grammys. And this year singer-songwriter John Mayer, 33, deserved an All-Time TMI ("too much information") Award, for a March *Playboy* interview. He was gracious about ex Jennifer Aniston ("the most communicative, sweetest, kindest person") but blurted about former love Jessica Simpson, "It was like . . . sexual napalm." Beyond that there's much that isn't printable here, except his lifetime ambition ("my biggest dream is to write pornography") and perhaps a blast of self-awareness: "I am a very . . . I'm just very, V-E-R-Y. And if you can't handle *very*, then I'm a douche bag."

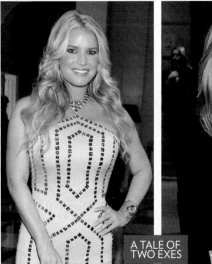

A TALE OF TWO EXES

Mayer on the power of Jessica Simpson: "Did you ever say, 'I want to quit my life and just . . . snort you?'"

"I'll always be sorry it didn't last," said Mayer of his year of off-and-on-again dating with Jennifer Aniston.

Pay-to-Play Royal

SHOW ME THE MONEY

THERE HAD been scandals in the past—some toe-sucking pictures come to mind—but this one had no edge of laughter. In a sting set up by the British tabloid *News of the World,* Sarah Ferguson, Duchess of York, was caught on video accepting a bribe of $40,000—with the promise that $700,000 more would be wired to her bank account—in return for her promise to introduce a purported "wealthy businessman" to her former husband, Prince Andrew. On the video, Fergie, 51, can be seen staring in delight at the pile of cash and heard saying the payments would "open up all the channels. . . . You meet Andrew."

Caught green-handed, the duchess, who is reportedly $6 million in debt, was abject. "I very deeply regret the situation and the embarrassment caused," she said. "It is true my financial situation is under stress. However, that is no excuse for a serious lapse in judgment."

"She's devastated," said a friend. "The fact that she would sink to that shows how desperate she is."

NEW YORK POST Page Six
LATE CITY FINAL

Oh, Bay-by!
Jason, Mets jolt Yanks SEE SPORTS

ROYAL BRIBE SHOCK
Fergie in 750G 'prince' sting

NEWS OF THE WORLD EXCLUSIVE

DUCHESS IN DUTCH

Despite headlines, the scandal, one royal watcher said, was unlikely to wreck Fergie's relationship with her ex: "Andrew is very much 'She's the mother of my children. She can do no wrong.'"

The heat in the mine was stifling. The two-month drama involved scores of workers and drew 1,500 journalists.

"PHOENIX" RISING

For more than two months, families lit candles and prayed. On day 17 a probe found the miners alive. On day 65 a high-tech rig completed a hole 28 inches in diameter—just wide enough to haul up one man at a time aboard a custom-made cage christened the Phoenix, after the mythical bird that rose from the ashes.

AS THE WORLD
WATCHED

The 33 men were dead—or so their loved ones feared until, 17 days after a collapse at the San José mine in Copiapó, Chile, a probe lowered down a bore hole found them alive 2,050 feet below the surface. With that, an unprecedented rescue kicked into gear. First the miners were provided with nutrient drinks; gradually the menu expanded to yogurt, cereal, tea, sandwiches, kiwis and rice. (Beans were held back for just the reason you'd think when 33 men are living in a confined space.) Over time the men were able to send messages, pictures and video to their families.

Meanwhile, engineers, to increase their chance of success, began drilling three separate rescue shafts. The job, many feared, might take six months. Instead, a high-tech oil drill did the job in less than half the time. (UPS air shipped more than 50,000 lbs. of drilling equipment from Pennsylvania for free.) Just after midnight on Oct. 13, after being trapped for 69 days, miner Florencio Avalos, 31, was hauled to the surface in a specially designed metal cage. Church bells rang throughout Chile, and millions watched, live on TV, around the world.

"We made a promise never to surrender," said Chilean President Sebastián Piñera, who stayed at the site until the last man reached the surface, less than 24 hours later. "And we kept it."

ANGEL
BEATS
COUGAR

Austin Forman, 11, was gathering firewood when the cougar charged. The boy's golden retriever, Angel, leaped at the animal as Austin ran into the house, where his mother, Sherri, dialed 911. Police arrived in minutes at the family's Boston Bar, British Columbia, home and shot the cat; Angel, bloodied and seemingly lifeless, lay on the ground. "Then, the next thing we knew," says Sherri, "she sucked in this big breath of air."

A week later—stitched, stapled and recovering well from two dozen puncture wounds—Angel came home from the vet and, as expected, leaped all over Austin. Neighbors dropped by with bones and treats, local police hailed Angel as a hero, and Austin's grandfather built her a new doghouse "with an insulated floor," said Austin. "She's going to be spoiled rotten from now on."

FOLLOW
THAT CAT!

Cat and mouse:
a portrait of the
author at work.

A FELINE WITH a strong personality, Sockington, by May, had 1.5 million Twitter followers (or about triple the number of Tom Cruise). The cat's thoughts—his owner, historian Jason Scott, 40, handles the tedium of typing—about eating, napping and feeling superior to Scott have even drawn interest from literary agents—who've been, so far, rebuffed. "I'd rather people say, 'Remember Sockington the cat?'" says Scott, "than 'remember Sockington? He was really good until that book.'"

Unfazed by fame, Sockington prefers to focus on what's really important: "For example I still lack a bed made of salmon."

MY (VERY)
LITTLE PONY

BORN APRIL 22 to two miniature horses, 14-in.-tall Einstein is believed to be the world's smallest equine. A YouTube video of his first shaky steps has drawn more than a million hits, and more than 4,000 people lined up in the rain to get a look at him during an open house at the Tiz A Miniature Horse Farm in Barnstead, N.H. Vets say his size is not a defect, just a rare lineup of the right genes. Said one delighted visitor: "I could have stuck him in my purse."

Bantam buckaroo: a visitor says hi to Einstein.

Star

FABSOLUTELY
AB-ULOUS

THE GUYS AT Miami's Imperial Club retirement community—plus an interloper, Mike "the Situation" Sorrentino, there filming a segment of *Jersey Shore*—took it off for the camera. Sure, Mike may have won the bathing suit part of the competition, but later the Imperials beat him silly at Canasta.

Tracks

That's Gross, Man

TOM CRUISE

FAUX PATE buffed and chest wig fluffed, Tom Cruise revived his memorable *Tropic Thunder* character—sweaty, expletive-snapping Hollywood producer Les Grossman—in a surprise opening dance number with Jennifer Lopez at the MTV Movie Awards.

Going for broke, Cruise enthusiastically . . .

. . . shook his money-maker and, metaphorically speaking . . .

. . . spilled change all over the floor.

'SCUSE ME, WHILE I KISS THE SKY

Have you ever been . . . experienced? Well, he has: Bill Murray channeled his inner Jimi Hendrix at a guitar fest in June.

JACKIE ALMOST?

No doubt there *will* be a pillbox hat: Demure in white gloves and baby blue, Katie Holmes filmed *The Kennedys* for the History Channel.

WET 'N' MILD

Kingston, 4 (foreground, with a pal), and Zuma, 2 (above), sons of singers Gwen Stefani and Gavin Rossdale, hit the sand in Newport Beach, Calif., in their shorts of many colors.

WATER BUGS

Come summer, lucky kids, including celebrity offspring, hit the beach. A year after their father's passing, Michael Jackson's children retreated to Hawaii (right). "They still feel the loss of not having their father," said a source. "They miss him tremendously, but they have grown stronger."

Michael Jackson's oldest, Prince Michael I, 13, seemed to take a modified Zen approach.

BEACH BOY

Maddox Pitt-Jolie, 9, frolicked with the fam in Malibu and later, boogie-boarding, caught a wave and was sitting on top of the world.

Side-slider Paris, 12, "is like a little mother" with her sibs, said a source.

Prince Michael II, a.k.a. "Blanket," "is still shy," said the source, "but he's way more outgoing than he used to be."

What's got three wheels and flies? John Cusack, presumably, on his BRP Can-Am Spyder in L.A. "It was so easy to operate," he said of his new toy. "It was like I had been riding for years."

BYE-BYE
BEARDIE

A FAMOUS GREEK, Alcibiades, once cropped the tail of his otherwise handsome dog hoping that Athenians would focus on *that* and stop gossiping about the rest of his life. Maybe that was the theory behind Brad Pitt's scruffy, occasionally beaded, never-explained beard, which, for more than a year, inspired fevered comment before disappearing, modestly and without fanfare, in July. Angelina Jolie was fine with the Boho look. "I love Brad in every state," she told *Vanity Fair*.

BEFORE

AFTER

WHO'S THAT GIRL?

Yes, they do grow up fast. One year they're in pigtails, the next they're launching a clothing line at Macy's. Okay, maybe not *every* kid—but that *was* the case for Madonna's daughter Lourdes, 14, who suddenly seems very grown up.

With mom Madonna at a benefit in Manhattan in April 2010.

In plaid, with dad Carlos Leon in 2003.

Going to a Kabbalah service in New York, 2004.

At brother Rocco's London birthday in 2006, age 10.

Multitasking in Manhattan in 2009.

Prince Harry had a great fall . . .

. . . but fortunately was still able to enjoy his summer.

UN-HORSED
HARRY

MY KINGDOM FOR a horse—that's somewhat more cooperative? On a visit to the former colonies, Britain's Prince Harry, 26, took a tumble while playing in a charity polo match on Governor's Island in New York harbor. With only his pride bruised, he was soon back in the saddle and eventually scored three goals for his team as part of an exciting, if unsuccessful, effort against a squad led by Argentina's Nacho Figueras, perhaps the best-known player in the world. The match, sponsored by Veuve Clicquot champagne, raised money for children suffering from AIDS in the African nation of Lesotho.

"DISCREET AND DIGNIFIED"

Middleton (with William in Scotland last May) has shown the royal family "she will make a fantastic princess," says a friend.

THROTTLE JOCKEY

On a ski trip with Middleton's family in the French Alps in March, William kiddingly called her father "Dad."

Harry bounced back quickly— and almost literally.

A NATION
EXHALES

I'M ONLY 22 FOR God's sake," Prince William once told a reporter. "I don't want to get married until I'm at least 28!" That birthday came and went on June 21, and the prince and Kate Middleton, 28, his girlfriend of eight years, kept maddeningly mum. And then . . . strike up the band! Cue the royal herald! On Nov. 16, Buckingham Palace announced that William had proposed and Kate had said—surprise!—yes.

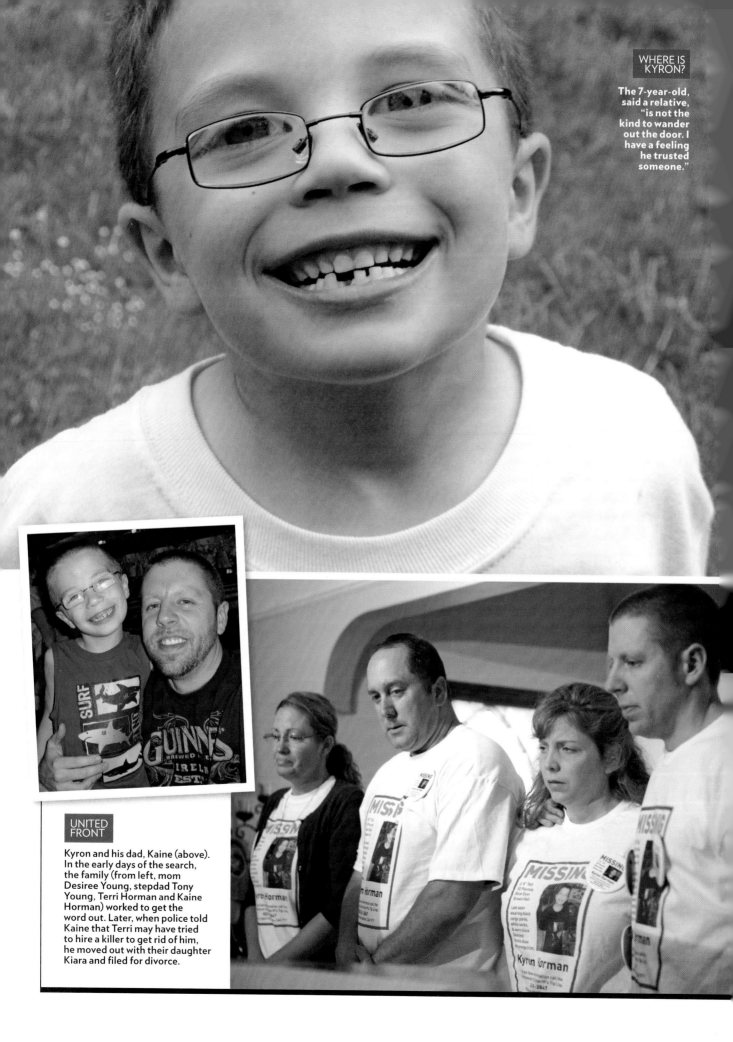

The 7-year-old, said a relative, "is not the kind to wander out the door. I have a feeling he trusted someone."

UNITED FRONT

Kyron and his dad, Kaine (above). In the early days of the search, the family (from left, mom Desiree Young, stepdad Tony Young, Terri Horman and Kaine Horman) worked to get the word out. Later, when police told Kaine that Terri may have tried to hire a killer to get rid of him, he moved out with their daughter Kiara and filed for divorce.

Crime

LOHAN SPIRALS, LETTERMAN GETS JUSTICE, AND THE DISAPPEARANCE OF A PORTLAND 7-YEAR-OLD RAISES TROUBLING, AND SO FAR UNANSWERED, QUESTIONS

Kyron Horman

MISSING BOY

Last seen at Skyline Elementary School, Portland, OR
Friday, June 4, 2010

KYRON HORMAN

Age - 7 yrs old

Height - 3'8' * Weight - 50 lbs

Eye color - Blue * Hair - Brown

Last seen wearing black cargo pants, white socks, black Sketcher shoes with orange trim.

PLEASE call the Multnomah County Sheriff's tip line with any information.

503-261-2847

URGENT information please call - 911

A police flyer. Friends of stepmom Terri Horman say any suspicion she is involved is misplaced. "I never heard her say, 'my stepson,'" says one. "She says, 'I miss my son.'"

MYSTERY OF A MISSING CHILD

A bespectacled 7-year-old with a big grin, Kyron Horman arrived early on June 4 at Skyline School, just outside Portland, Ore., to tour the science fair and pose proudly in front of his project, a diorama of red-eyed tree frogs. His stepmom, Terri Horman, 40, said she last saw him walking toward class at 8:45 a.m. When she met his bus at 3:30 p.m., he wasn't onboard. A frantic call to the school revealed that he had been marked absent. He has not been seen since.

The tragedy and mystery have only deepened. Although Terri has never been named a suspect or a person of interest, police have interviewed her repeatedly, distributed flyers with pictures of her and the type of white Ford F250 truck she drives, and given her at least two polygraph tests (results have not been released). Friends said any suspicion was misplaced. "She's a mess," said one. "She sends me text messages and says, 'I miss my son. I want my son back.' It's heartbreaking to talk to her."

Then, on June 26, came a bizarre twist: According to *The Oregonian,* police told Kyron's father, Kaine Horman, 36, that a local landscaper had claimed that, months before, Terri had offered him money to kill Kaine. Kaine moved out of the house immediately with the couple's daughter Kiara, 18 months, got a restraining order and filed for divorce. As the investigation plays out, Kaine is focusing on hope. "I'm just trying to get the house ready for when Kyron comes home," he says. "Hopefully it's tomorrow, or today. Hopefully it's right now."

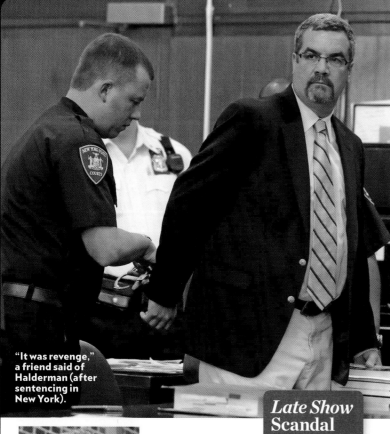

"It was revenge," a friend said of Halderman (after sentencing in New York).

DAVE'S DATE

Ex-staffer Stephanie Birkitt "is sweet, goofy and quirky, which is a major allure for David," said a *Late Show* insider.

LETTERMAN & THE LAW

DAVID LETTERMAN guarded his privacy for years, but that abruptly ended in October '09 with his on-air admission that he "had sex with women who work for me." That same day, former CBS News producer Robert "Joe" Halderman was arrested for trying to extort $2 million from the *Late Show* host by threatening to expose his infidelities, including an alleged affair with his ex-girlfriend Stephanie Birkitt, a Letterman assistant.

Halderman was sentenced to six months for attempted grand larceny and was barred from contacting Letterman until 2018. Letterman began repairing his marriage to Regina Lasko, mother of their 7-year-old son Harry, whom he dated for 20 years before he wed hermarrying in 2009. In April, Letterman sounded hopeful that his family life can "even be better, in a different way," and his *Late Show* ratings have not suffered. In July, Halderman was nominated for an Emmy for producing a *48 Hours Mystery* segment about the Italian murder trial of American exchange student Amanda Knox. (He didn't win.)

SHEEN ERUPTS

MY HUSBAND had me with a knife," Brooke Mueller said in a Dec. 25, 2009, 911 call. "I was scared for my life." Mueller also claimed her husband, actor Charlie Sheen, then 44, told her, "I have ex-police I can hire and know how to get the job done, and they won't leave a trace."

Sheen, no stranger to trouble, was arrested; in August he pleaded guilty to a misdemeanor assault charge and was sentenced to 30 days in rehab and 30 days probation. Earlier in the year, Mueller, then 32, had also sought help for a substance abuse issue. In November, after he was caught in yet another mess, Sheen filed for divorce.

Sheen is seeking joint physical and legal custody of the couple's 1½-year-old twin boys, Bob and Max.

"I said when he was let loose the first time, 'This is not the end of his criminal career,'" said Dave Holloway, Natalee's father.

FLORES RAMIREZ

"She was having a beautiful life," Ricardo Flores said of daughter Stephany, a business administration student. Surveillance photos showed Flores entering the Hotel Tac lobby behind van der Sloot.

Holloway Suspect

VAN DER SLOOT
BEHIND BARS

Arrested twice but never charged with Natalee Holloway's 2005 disappearance in Aruba, Joran van der Sloot, 23, will likely stay behind bars after confessing to the murder of Peruvian college student Stephany Flores Ramirez, 21, who had been found bloodied, with her neck broken, in a Lima hotel on May 30. Chillingly, that was five years to the day that Holloway vanished during a graduation trip.

Peruvian authorities possess a trove of potentially damning video evidence: van der Sloot and Flores playing poker at the same table at the Atlantic City Casino in Miraflores; van der Sloot and Flores entering room 309 of the Hotel Tac together; van der Sloot leaving the room alone more than three hours later, toting a suitcase and backpack. It's unclear how the murder investigation in Peru will affect the Holloway case, but "he's not going to get away from this one like he did with my sister," said Natalee's brother Matt Holloway, 22. While he's awaiting trial, van der Sloot is being held in a grimy, 10-ft.-by 8-ft. cell. If convicted he could be facing a 35-year sentence.

HOLLOWAY

"She was devastated this could happen again," said a spokeswoman for Natalee's mother.

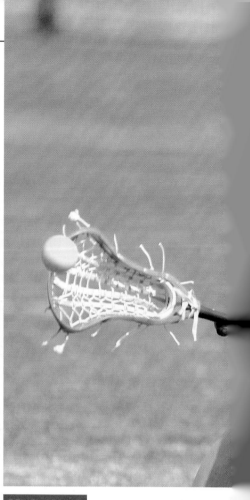

REMEMBERING YEARDLEY

The UVA senior (left, and above, in 2009) "loved life and lived it to the fullest, always with a big smile," said her mother, Sharon. Added friend Lindsay Smith: "Her last name pretty much said it all."

Yeardley Love

MURDER AT UVA

On the lacrosse field, University of Virginia senior Yeardley Love was a fleet defensive player known for her stick skills and sunny disposition. "No matter what you asked her to do, she did it with the biggest smile," says her former UVA coach Amy Appell. Weeks away from graduation, Love, 22, was hoping to close out her college career representing the Cavaliers at the NCAA tournament. But on May 3, tragedy struck: Love was found murdered in her off-campus apartment, the victim of a brutal physical assault. Within hours police arrested her ex-boyfriend George Huguely, a 6'2", 209-lb. senior and fellow lacrosse player.

Troubling details about the couple

Charged with murder: ex-boyfriend George Huguely.

soon emerged. Students say Huguely's aggressive behavior was triggered by alcohol—he had been arrested in 2008 for intoxication and received a six-month probation—and stories circulated that he'd fought with Love a few days before her death. Though school officials say they were unaware of any problems, students criticized an elite lacrosse culture that did little to curb bad-boy excesses. Still, male lacrosse players carried Love's casket down the aisle of Baltimore's Cathedral of Mary Our Queen during a May 8 memorial service that drew more than 1,500 mourners. As Huguely, charged with murder, awaits trial, Love's classmates wonder if they could have done more to stop the abuse. "Her friends," says Danielle Hayes, a junior, "should have said, 'Go to the authorities. This is not okay.'"

UVA's lacrosse team mourned Love at an emotional memorial service in May.

Accused murderer Amy Bishop in March.

KILLER
PROFESSOR

HUMILIATED after being denied tenure at the University of Alabama, Amy Bishop, 45—a biology professor and Harvard Ph.D. who trumpeted her Ivy League pedigree—opened fire at a biology-faculty meeting on Feb. 12 with a 9mm pistol, killing three colleagues and wounding three others.

Soon afterward disturbing details began to emerge about her life: In Massachusetts, at an IHOP, she had once punched a woman who had taken the last child booster seat, and a professor recalled that she had become enraged when told she wouldn't be the lead writer on a scientific paper. "I never saw an explosion like that," he said. Most shocking of all: 24 years before, Bishop's brother Seth had died when, police decided at the time, she accidentally fired their father's shotgun. The Alabama shooting caused that case to be reopened. In June she was indicted for Seth's murder as well.

THE BOOKING ALBUM

Lohan mug shots (clockwise, from top left): arrested for drunk driving and cocaine possession, (2007); jailed for two DUIs (2007); jailed for skipping alcohol classes (2010); jailed for failing a drug test (2010).

Troubled Actress

LINDSAY
LOHAN

IT IS, PERHAPS, the most public, relentlessly documented decline in Hollywood history. In the digital age, it sometimes seems as if Lindsay Lohan's every drug test, paparazzi scuffle, traffic stop, court appearance and public denial is reported—if not tweeted by Lohan herself—in real time. Yet it continues: The tally now comes to three stints in jail, three ankle-monitoring bracelets and four trips to rehab for the former Disney actress, who turned 24 in July.

Her mother, Dina, 48, seems to be in denial, telling the *Today* show's Matt Lauer on Aug. 13 that Lindsay's struggles were "blown out of proportion." Friends say anyone who confronts the star is frozen out: "When I said, as did many people, 'We will not stand idly by and watch you totally destroy yourself,' is when she stopped being honest with me," said one.

And, despite everything, Lindsay herself seems unable, or unwilling, to deal with the slow-motion train wreck that has become her life. "She will have a moment of clarity and say things like, 'My life is a mess. What have I done?'" said a friend. "But those moments are short, and they don't stick. She drifts off into crazy land, thinking she's done nothing wrong and everyone is out to get her."

COPS NAB
BRAZEN TEEN

FOR TWO YEARS he played cat and mouse with police as his notoriety grew, but on July 11, Colton Harris-Moore—known as the Barefoot Bandit for deliberately leaving his footprints and, sometimes, drawings of bare feet at crime scenes—was finally collared in a chase straight out of *James Bond*. The 19-year-old self-taught pilot had hot-wired a Cessna in Indiana, flown 1,000 miles and crash-landed in the Bahamas, then tried a water escape before cops nabbed him by shooting the engine of his stolen boat.

Harris-Moore's flair for the dramatic may explain why the gangly 6'5" teen became a folk-cult hero, with 20,000 fans on a Facebook page; a movie deal is reportedly in the works. Following deportation from the Bahamas, Harris-Moore has disappeared once more—this time to a federal detention center in Seattle, where he is awaiting a formal indictment.

A THIEF'S CALLING CARD?

Chalk drawings of bare feet appeared on the floor of an Orcas Island, Wash., grocery store in February. Harris-Moore is suspected of more than 65 crimes.

Nancy (with her late father) has called the manslaughter charge "unjustified."

Nancy Kerrigan

COPING

Mark (top), said his lawyer, "did not cause the death of his father." Above: Brenda and Nancy at the funeral.

FAMILY **TRAUMA**

SHE WAS AN Olympic skating star, but her older brother, a 45-year-old plumber, had done jail time for drunk driving and for attacking his wife.

On Jan. 24, police responding to a 911 call found Daniel Kerrigan, 70, Nancy and Mark Kerrigan's father, unconscious in his kitchen. He was rushed to a hospital and pronounced dead. Mark, who had been living in the basement, told police that he put his hands on his father's neck during a fight. On Feb. 9, authorities determined the death was a homicide, and Mark was charged with manslaughter.

Mark's lawyer said that Daniel Kerrigan had heart problems unknown to his wife, Brenda, or son. Both Brenda and Nancy have said they will do whatever they can to help Mark. Said Brenda: "He's my son. My husband would not like what's going on in the courts."

I DO, A LOT

Finley with Cory Wynne in '04 (left) and Air Force reservist Ben Giles in '05. "She has no heart," said one ex. "The devil himself ain't got nothing on her."

TOO MANY HUSBANDS

"OF ALL THE THINGS she knew how to steal," said husband No.1, Jacob Anderson, "the worst was your heart." Other exes—at least 12 and perhaps as many as 39, most of them servicemen—say Bobbi Finley, 35, showered them with love then emptied their checking accounts. "I wanted to help," says one, who claims Finley told him she needed to marry quickly to qualify for a huge inheritance. "I feel like the biggest idiot in the world." Arrested in New Orleans, Finley said, "I do have issues, but I'm not a grifter."

"Monica was the axis around which our whole family revolved," Bruce (with Monica, in L.A. in 2002) said in a statement.

MURDER
IN MEXICO

After months of turmoil in their marriage, Bruce and Monica Beresford-Redman flew to Cancun with their two kids for what she hoped would be a relationship-saving vacation. But just days after checking into the plush Moon Palace Resort, something went horribly wrong. On April 6, the morning after several guests claim they heard the couple having a heated argument, Bruce, 38, a former Survivor producer, reported his wife missing. Two days later, on what would have been Monica's 42nd birthday, her body was found in a sewer.

Mexican authorities quickly determined that she had been asphyxiated and struck in the right temple—and, just as quickly, they turned their focus on Bruce. Given the scratches on his face and arms, plus the couple's alleged turbulent history, police briefly detained Bruce before releasing him on the condition that he not leave the country.

But on May 23, Beresford-Redman was back in L.A.—despite having had his passport seized by Mexican authorities—and filed to regain legal control over his kids Camila, 5, and Alec, 3, who had been placed under the temporary guardianship of his parents. (Monica's sister Carla, 46, has also been seeking guardianship.) On May 31, Mexican authorities issued a warrant for his arrest and plan to seek extradition. If Beresford-Redman fights to stay, it's unclear if or when he would be returned to Mexico. Meanwhile, Monica's family is hoping for justice. Says her father, João Burgos Filho: "I want the person who committed this heinous crime to be convicted."

THE FAMILY

Monica (with Camila and Alec) "lived for her kids," said her friend Mariza Alyrio. "I feel destroyed inside," said Monica's dad, João (below, with her sisters Carla, left, and Jeane in L.A. in May).

On May 31, Mexican authorities issued an arrest warrant for the former *Survivor* producer (left). "The children, they lost a mother," said Monica's sister Carla. "Now they could lose a father, It's very sad."

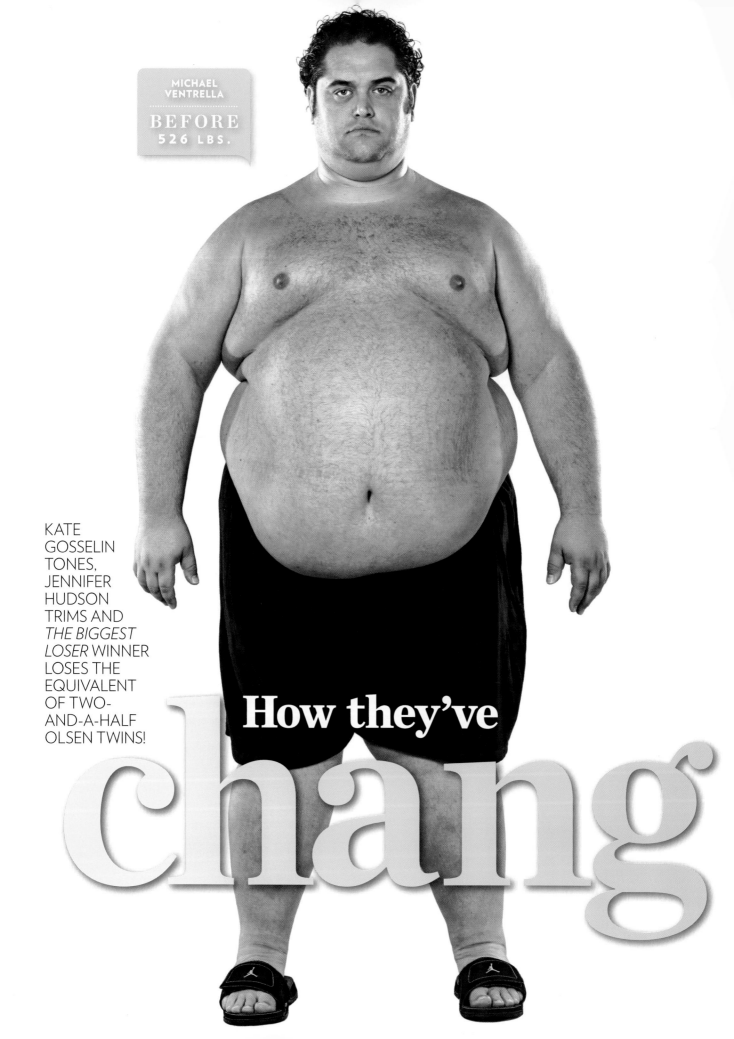

MICHAEL VENTRELLA

BEFORE
526 LBS.

KATE GOSSELIN TONES, JENNIFER HUDSON TRIMS AND *THE BIGGEST LOSER* WINNER LOSES THE EQUIVALENT OF TWO-AND-A-HALF OLSEN TWINS!

How they've

chang

MICHAEL
VENTRELLA
....
AFTER
262 LBS.

ed

BIGGEST
LOSER *EVER*

A s a deejay, Michael Ventrella didn't stop the party when the club closed down. "I'd stay and get a couple of cocktails, then I'd order some greasy food," he says. "It was such a bad lifestyle."

Those days and nights are over. Formerly 526 lbs., the 6′3″ Chicago native lost a jaw-dropping 264 lbs. on *Biggest Loser*—the most in the show's nine-season history. Ventrella, 32, now gets up early to go on six-mile bike rides and eats homemade pizza with low-fat cheese. But some old habits are hard to break: He still catches himself walking down corridors sideways. And when he picks up new 38″-waist pants, his first reaction is, "'This will fit a Ken doll.' But then I'll button them and be blown away," says Ventrella. "I feel reborn."

Kate Plus Eight Star

KATE **GOSSELIN**

B ody after baby is one thing. Body after eight babies—sextuplets, plus two more—is something else all together. Nonetheless, Kate Gosselin says that with the exception of a tummy-tuck following the birth of Aaden, Alexis, Collin, Hannah, Joel and Leah, now 6, she got where she is without surgery, weird pharmaceuticals or even a trainer. Early in the summer, she says, "I started wondering if I could run as far as this one spot near my house. . . . So I did, and each day I just kept going. Now I'm thinking I'll be happy when I can do 10 miles three times a week."

Add a sensible diet—"I've always eaten healthy, but I also pay attention to how much I'm eating too"—and four months later the results were such that Gosselin, 35, was willing, nay, eager, to pose in a bikini. "My kids will hug me and say, 'Your stomach is very hard, mama.' I just say, 'Thank you!'" Refreshingly, Gosselin admits she's not doing all this for her health. Or, not *only* for her health: "I'm waiting for Mr. Right," she says. "It would be nice if somebody noticed me, sure! . . . All I can say to this mystery man is hurry it up!" Meanwhile she'll sweat and hope. "I still look in the mirror and see plenty I want to change," she says. "And that's why the next day, no matter what the weather or how tired I feel, I get up, and I run again."

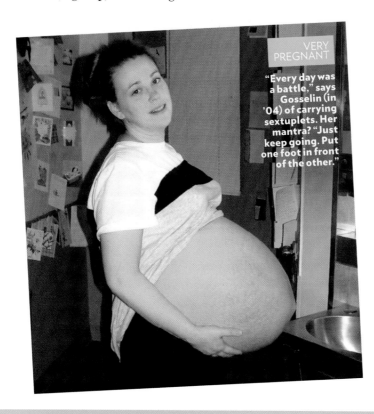

VERY
PREGNANT

"Every day was a battle," says Gosselin (in '04) of carrying sextuplets. Her mantra? "Just keep going. Put one foot in front of the other."

"After my first run," says Gosselin of her regimen, "I felt like a totally new person."

SOME DAYS I
THINK 'I CAN'T
DO THIS.'
THEN I TELL
MYSELF, 'YOU
CAN AND
YOU WILL.'"

HAPPY HUDSON

JENNIFER HUDSON, 29, began losing weight to play Winnie Mandela in a movie and just kept going—becoming, along the way, a spokeswoman for Weight Watchers. After years of faddish diets, the singer-actress now pays more attention to portions and hits the gym regularly. "I'm a cardio maniac!" she says. The result? She dropped from a size 16 to a 6—and is thrilled. "This is the way I want to be," she says, "and the way I want to stay!"

"I don't believe in shortcuts or drugs," Hudson has said of her weight-loss philosophy.

TREME TO TRIM

JOHN GOODMAN, 58, lost more than 100 lbs. by quitting drinking, cutting out sugar and, with a push from his trainer, hitting the gym six days a week. "I'm breaking a sweat," he says, "but I'm not going nuts."

Basically he just got tired of the way he had been living. "I know it sounds sappy, but it was a waste," said the actor, who most recently appeared in *Treme*. "It takes a lot of creative energy to sit on your ass and figure out what you're going to eat next. I wanted to live better."

"I just ordered some nice slacks," said a proud Goodman. "I finally got them, and they're too big now!"

DRAW DREW THINNER

DREW CAREY didn't *like* being big. "It sucks," says the 52-year-old actor. "I was diabetic with type 2 diabetes." After Carey embarked on a strict regimen, shaving his diet of carbohydrates— "not even a cracker"— and hitting the gym regularly, he dropped 80 lbs. in about six months. "I'm not diabetic anymore," he says. "No medication."

As for how he keeps at it: "Once I started dropping a couple pant sizes, it was easy. You see the results, then you don't wanna stop."

"I like being skinny," says Carey. "I was sick of being fat on camera."

SO LONG, TWINKIES

JASON ALEXANDER, 51, became the latest celebrity spokesman for Jenny Craig and in his first four weeks lost 12 lbs. toward a goal of 30. "My younger son has a nickname for me: SFB— short, fat, bald," says the 5'5" actor. "I said to him, 'You're going to have to make it just SB pretty soon!'"

Alexander exercises regularly and cut his daily caloric intake. After a year in the program, his weight is now 165.

"Twinkies," Alexander says, "were one of my favorites."

BEFORE
....
Nov. 20, 2009

"For the past three years," she said, "I thought about what to have done."

Heidi Montag 2.0

TOO MUCH?

"I AM," SAID Heidi Montag, "absolutely beyond obsessed."

No one—with the possible exception of Joan Rivers—would disagree. On Nov. 20, 2009, Montag, 24, who was a regular on *The Hills,* walked into the Beverly Hills office of plastic surgeon Dr. Frank Ryan and in 10 hours had 10 procedures, including breast augmentation, nose job, chin reduction and liposuction. Why on earth? "I would say the biggest reason is to feel better, to feel perfect," she said. "People said I had a Jay Leno chin, they'd circle it on blogs, and . . . it bothered me. On *The Hills,* my ears would be sticking out like Dumbo."

When she posed for *Playboy* in 2009, she added, "I didn't fill out the bras, and they had to Photoshop my boobs bigger, and it was so disheartening. I almost cried." Although Dr. Ryan put in "the most he could put in this time," said Montag, "I'm already planning my next surgery. I'm determined to get bigger ones! I just love boobs."

She says her husband, Spencer Pratt, 27, tried to talk her out of the surgeries ("No, Heidi, you are so beautiful; this is out of control") and that her mother, upon seeing the results for the first time, looked at her "like a zoo animal . . . a circus freak."

No matter. "We all want to feel attractive," said Montag, who says she is thrilled by the way she now looks. "So who is anyone to judge me?"

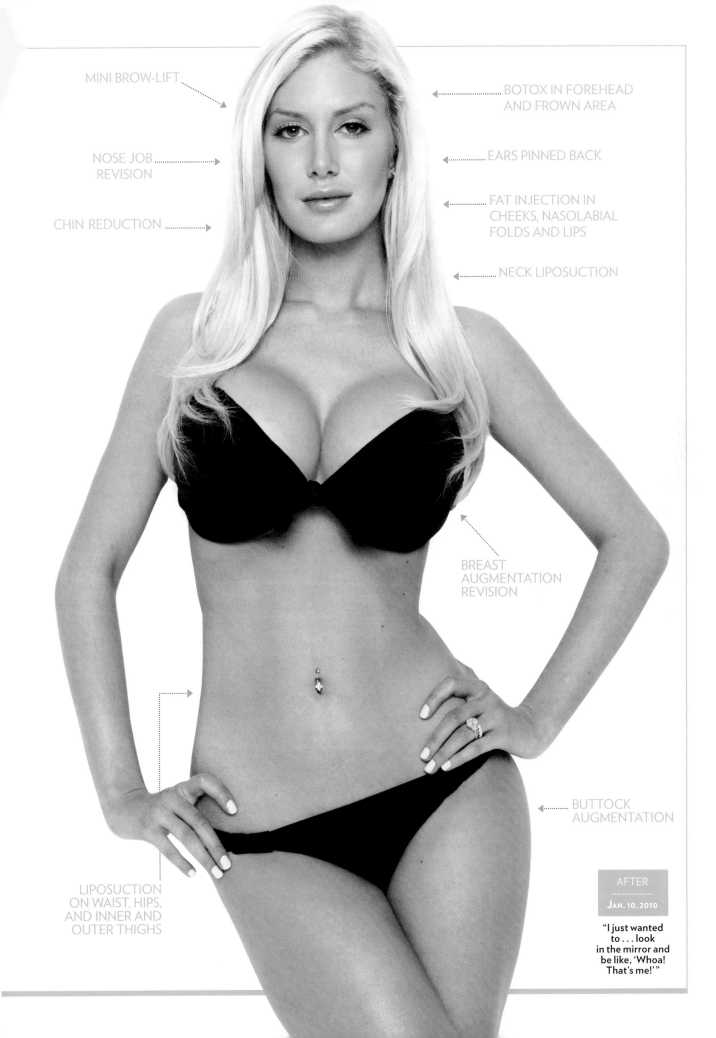

MINI BROW-LIFT

NOSE JOB
REVISION

CHIN REDUCTION

BOTOX IN FOREHEAD
AND FROWN AREA

EARS PINNED BACK

FAT INJECTION IN
CHEEKS, NASOLABIAL
FOLDS AND LIPS

NECK LIPOSUCTION

BREAST
AUGMENTATION
REVISION

BUTTOCK
AUGMENTATION

LIPOSUCTION
ON WAIST, HIPS,
AND INNER AND
OUTER THIGHS

AFTER

JAN. 10, 2010

"I just wanted
to . . . look
in the mirror and
be like, 'Whoa!
That's me!'"

Movies

TOY STORY 3

THE CREATORS at Pixar play pop culture like a piano and produce music that sounds like nothing else. From joyously metrosexual Ken ("Love your leg warmers!") to Lots-O'-Huggin' Bear—a corrupt prison warden reimagined as a plush pink ursine who smells of strawberries—*Toy Story 3*, layered, funny and emotional, once again turned toys into characters audiences cared about. A *lot*: By November the movie had grossed nearly $1.1 billion—the most of any movie in 2010 and more than any animated film ever. Strong, manly critics admitted crying at the end. Said A.O. Scott of the *New York Times*: "This film—this whole three-part, 15-year epic—about the adventures of a bunch of silly plastic junk turns out also to be a long, melancholy meditation on loss, impermanence and the noble, stubborn, foolish thing called love."

JULIA ATE, PRAYED AND LOVED, LEO GOT INTO PEOPLE'S HEADS, STALLONE HAD AN ACTION HIT (AT 64!)—BUT IT WAS BUZZ & CO WHO EARNED $1 BILLION

INCEPTION

A worthy successor to *The Matrix* in the Alternate Realities Sweepstakes, *Inception*—a corporate-espionage caper involving the invasion and manipulation of dreams—mixed a clever plot with super CGI, en route to earning more than $815 million.

THE SOCIAL NETWORK

What if 500 million people showed up at a party and no one knew the host? That's part of the draw of *Network*, a look at the life of Facebook billionaire Mark Zuckerberg, 26. Is he an amoral nerd who betrays friends to get to the top? A visionary laser-focused on helping people communicate? Both? Viewers are left to debate (Director David Fincher says the film is fiction; screenwriter Aaron Sorkin calls it nonfiction). Zuckerberg himself opted for diversion: A week before *The Social Network* premiered, he donated $100 million to Newark schools.

Julia & pachyderm

Sly, Rourke & Hog

GUYS VS. GELATO

ONE WAS a sensitive search for meaning, explored through food, spirituality and love. The other . . . not so much. But when the much-anticipated *Eat, Pray, Love*, starring a radiant Julia Roberts and based on Elizabeth Gilbert's Oprah-backed bestselling book, opened against Sylvester Stallone's *The Expendables*—believed to be history's 2,117th misfits-on-a-mission movie—guns and testosterone beat romance and tagliatelli hands down. Final score (box office through October): *Pray*: $181 million. Sly: $257 million.

HEARTBREAK KIDS

HAVING WON an Oscar for *An Inconvenient Truth*, director Davis Guggenheim tackled another not-obviously-ripe-for-the-multiplex topic—improving public education—in *Waiting for Superman*. By focusing on the fates of real kids waiting to hear if they've won a lottery slot in a good school. *Superman*, a likely Oscar nominee, leads audiences, said one critic, through "waves of despair, hope, outrage, and finally, constructive, motivating anger."

WOBBLY ROM-COMS!

Boy meets girl. Boy loses girl. Boy . . . hey, I'm bored. Wanna go out for yogurt?

THE BACK-UP PLAN One of 2010's rich crop of weakish romantic comedies, Jennifer Lopez' ticking-clock tale got little love from critics.

THE BOUNTY HUNTER Reviewers carped about thudding clichés, but the Jennifer Aniston-Gerard Butler vehicle still made money worldwide.

KILLERS Nope, it's not "a monstrosity," concluded one critic of this Ashton Kutcher-Katherine Heigl starrer, "just an empty summer hodgepodge of . . . witlessness."

THE UNWATCHED

Yes, there were gobblers at the octoplex

THE A TEAM, Wolfman, Prince of Persia: The Sands of Time (right) and *The Sorcerer's Apprentice* were all big-budget disappointments, but only one film had the je ne sais quoi that may, in time, allow it to enter the American vocabulary as a verb. As in, "Why on earth did they spend all that money on such a patently boneheaded project?" "No idea. They totally *MacGruber*-ed."

SPLAT PACK!

Season 1 ended with a family portrait that devolved into a mud-slinging contest.

Televis

MODERN FAMILY

An old guy with a hot Latina wife? A gay couple with an adopted Asian daughter? A goofy dad who clearly doesn't always know best? Fifty years ago, in a *Leave It to Beaver* world, a show about the type of extended family on *Modern Family* would have been unthinkable. Nonetheless, the creators of TV's golden age would no doubt recognize their progeny: *Modern Family*'s farcical scripts are tight and funny—the No. 1 requirement of any great sitcom—and, above all, the show is kind. Mistakes are made, petty rivalries flare up, Colombian accents are made fun of ("It's not blessings in the skies, it's blessings in disguise!"), but most episodes end with a hug, virtual or real, and a not too painfully obvious lesson learned. Somewhere, Ward Cleaver, Ozzie Nelson, and Howard Cunningham—Richie's dad—are smiling.

ion

FAREWELL, *UGLY BETTY*. HELLO, BETTY WHITE! PLUS: *MODERN FAMILY* HITS ITS STRIDE, SIMON COWELL HITS THE ROAD, HURRICANE SNOOKI HITS MIAMI!

Gleek Victory

Ice, ice baby: Stars Jane Lynch and Matthew Morrison attack with slushies.

LET'S PUT ON A SHOW!

PERHAPS THE surest sign of *Glee*'s growing pop-cultural mojo was that fans were not ashamed to call themselves Gleeks. (MTV's *Jersey Shore* was a hit, too, but the adjective "Snookian" waits to be coined.) At its best, the FOX show approached the delirious heights of old movie musicals while sneaking in small amounts of postmillennial snark and irony. A shot-by-shot remake of Madonna's landmark "Vogue" video became a makeover of cheerleading coach Sue Sylvester (Emmy-winner Jane Lynch). Another episode was devoted to the music of Britney Spears (with a cameo by the star). None of this would have risen above camp if the show weren't somehow true to the sillinesses and sorrows of adolescence. In the same week, for instance, gay Kurt (Chris Colfer) sang a heartbreaking "I Want to Hold Your Hand" while less sensitive jock Finn (Cory Monteith) thought he saw Jesus on a grilled cheese sandwich.

The *Jersey* gang (above) and Snooki being arrested in July.

A SHORE-TO-SHORE CRAZE

In July President Obama tripped up when he said on *The View*, "I don't know who Snooki is." He'd made a joke reference to her in a prior speech! Who *didn't* know Snooki? In its second season, *Jersey Shore*, the MTV hit about "guidos" and "guidettes" so tanned they look wood-smoked, totally rocked the ratings. The 4'9" Snooki was the breakout, not too bright but appealingly honest. After a disorderly conduct arrest, she said, "Too many tequilas. What are you gonna do?" And Mike "the Situation" Sorrentino landed on ABC's *Dancing with the Stars*, thanks to six-pack abs and a philosophy of "GTL." That's "gym, tan, laundry," Mr. President.

THE WHITE ALBUM

At 88, Betty White, who starred in her first sitcom in 1952, was suddenly TV's "it"girl. The craze took off with her cameo in a Superbowl Snickers ad. That fueled a Facebook campaign to hire her to host *Saturday Night Live*—which she did May 8 (left), becoming the oldest host ever (and winning an Emmy). Then she landed a new sitcom, *Hot in Cleveland*. If most of her material played off hip young viewers' cute notions of senior citizens, so what? As she put it, "I'm still working my tail off."

LOSING
BETTY

In the words of *Project Runway* host Heidi Klum, "In fashion, one day you're in, the next you're out." And so *Ugly Betty,* ABC's campy fashion-world comedy starring America Ferrera (right), left the scene after four candy-colored seasons. ABC's *Lost* (below) got lost too. Prime time's most entertainingly baffling show, which began in 2004 with plane-crash survivors puzzling out how to live on a mysterious island, offered up a few answers in its controversial finale. Jack (Matthew Fox) had apparently died and entered the afterlife. (And a brief DVD epilogue explained why there were polar bears on that island.) The clock finally stopped on Kiefer Sutherland's antiterror thriller *24,* which premiered on FOX a few months after 9/11 in 2001. And NBC's *Law & Order,* which debuted in 1990, ceased and desisted—tied with *Gunsmoke*'s 20 seasons for the longest-running show ever.

JUGGLING
JUDGES

Goodbye to *American Idol* as we knew it: With the ninth season done, acerbic Simon Cowell departed, followed by Ellen DeGeneres and Kara DioGuardi. The 2011 *Idol* will bring back only Randy Jackson, along with new judges Steven Tyler and Jennifer Lopez.

Music

FASHION HAND-GRENADE LADY GAGA CONTINUES TO KEEP
SUBTLETY AT BAY; JUSTIN BIEBER RIDES THE TEEN IDOL TIGER

WHAT TO
WEAR?

SHOCK FROCKS

"I'm just trying to change the world," Lady Gaga said, "one sequin at a time."

ONE OF THESE days Lady Gaga will rock the fashion world and show up in . . . a Chanel suit? A little black dress? Bill Blass resort wear? Until then Gaga gawkers will have to make do with glampunk and glitter, with a healthy dose of Barbarella tossed in.

Her relentless pace of hit records—"Telephone" and "Alejandro" were international chart-toppers—and her can-you-top-this fashion cannot be easy; indeed, Gaga, 24, collapsed briefly during a March performance in Australia. "I passed out about three times onstage that night," she later told a local deejay. "The jet lag caught up with me."

Fans wait to find out what's next. "She's already larger than life," said a friend. "How do you get larger than that?"

SHOW
STOPPERS

Whacked by the economy, many big summer tours suffered from sudden cancellitis

Popular pop performer Perry, playful and pretty in pink.

FEW ACTS ever say they had trouble selling tickets—but the sheer number of canceled concert dates (Rihanna, above, was one of many acts that dialed back) suggested something was amiss. Industry sources and blogging fans blamed high ticket prices in a weak economy.

THE ALL-FEMALE Lilith Fair (above, from left, Jasmine Chadwick, Miranda Lambert, A Fine Frenzy and Sarah McLachlan) was forced to cancel shows. Cofounder Terry McBride called 2010 "one of the most challenging summer concert seasons."

THE JONAS BROTHERS dropped planned concerts in Denver, Nashville, Orlando, Charlotte, St. Louis and other cities.

THE GURL NEXT DOOR

Pop-music fans in search of a summer anthem had to look no further than Katy Perry's *Teenage Dream*, which spawned not one but *two* of the season's big hits: the title track as well as "California Gurls"—a song apparently best sung while wearing an electric-blue Bettie Page wig and a risqué cupcake bra. "Some days I just want to look beautiful," said Perry (the new Mrs. Russell Brand), 26, "and other days I want people to see me and say, 'I want to party with that girl. She looks like a ball of fun.'" But not everyone appreciates her playful style: *Sesame Street* scrapped a segment in which Perry serenaded Elmo after parents complained that her dress exposed too much cleavage.

Drake performing in Miami last September.

THE NEW GUY

One of the few top hip-hop stars whose life experience includes a Bar Mitzvah, Drake—born Aubrey Drake Graham in Toronto—saw his first studio album, *Thank Me Later*, debut at No. 1 on the Billboard 200. Other hip-hop rookies who made a splash in 2010: B.o.B (Bobby Ray Simmons Jr.), whose first single, "Nothin' on You," reached No. 1 in the U.S. and Great Britain; and Nicki Minaj, who at one point was on seven singles, including "Your Love," that made the Billboard Hot 100 chart simultaneously.

Bieber (performing in New York City, left) says women have tried to follow him, but notes, "Moms in their soccer vans don't really scare me."

JUSTIN**BIEBER**

OKAY, KIDS, HERE'S how you do it: 1) Enter a local singing competition at age 12 and place second. 2) Your mom posts YouTube videos of the event so friends and family can check it out. 3) *Other* people start checking it out. 4) A music exec checks it out, goes nuts, talks you and your mom into moving from Stratford, Ont., to Atlanta, Ga., for musical grooming. 5) You're so good that Usher and Justin Timberlake fight to sign you to their respective labels (a key step; *do not overlook*). 6) Sell millions of records to screaming, crying, fainting, sighing tween girls.

It worked for teenthrob-of-the-moment Justin Bieber, 16, who's now looking to expand into acting. *Leave it to Bieber*, anyone?

Weddi

Chelsea
CLINTON
&
Marc
MEZVINSKY

JULY 31, 2010
RHINEBECK, N.Y.

ngs

HERE COMES
THE BRIDE (IN
VERA WANG)

Former President
Clinton made two
promises to Chelsea:
that he would lose
weight before the
ceremony and that
he wouldn't cry. He
did fine with the
first, wavered on
the second.

They skipped the customary "something borrowed, something blue," but on the morning of his wedding day, the groom did put on something old: a frayed T-shirt he had worn nearly 17 years earlier when he first met his future bride. Chelsea Clinton was just 13 then, Marc Mezvinsky 16, both brought along to the annual political Renaissance weekend their parents attended in South Carolina. The two met again at Stanford and became friends; in 2005 they began dating. After that, Mezvinsky made sure to hold on to the shirt, he told nearly 500 wedding guests gathered at the Astor Courts estate in Rhinebeck, N.Y.

It was one of many romantic moments indicating how "meant-to-be" this union was. The couple "are not people who usually stand around grinning," said one guest. "But the whole weekend they radiated joy. No one doubted the strength of their feelings."

As a testament to those feelings, both families made sure the day was all about Marc and Chelsea and not, as it could have been, about networking. "The people coming are her friends and people who have been meaningful in her life," the mother of the bride, Secretary of State Hillary Clinton, 63, said days before. No Obamas were present, nor herds of Hollywood A-listers. Oprah? Nah. "This was Marc and Chelsea's list," said wedding planner Bryan Rafanelli. Guest Ted Danson, whose wife, Mary Steenburgen, is an old Clinton pal from Arkansas, joked accurately, "Are we the only celebrities here?"

"He's perfect," a friend said of Mezvinsky, a hedge fund trader. "He comes from a loving family. He really has her back." The 4-ft.-tall cake, gluten-free but not fat-free, required 50 lbs. of sugar, 30 lbs. of butter and 360 eggs. Hillary Clinton's mother, Dorothy Rodham, 91 (left, with the Secretary of State and Chelsea), helped plan the wedding.

Country Bride

Carrie UNDERWOOD
&
Mike FISHER

JULY 10, 2010
GREENSBORO, GA.

A small-town Oklahoma girl turned country superstar, Carrie Underwood has already led a storybook life. But moments before the singer walked down the aisle to exchange vows with her Canadian hockey-pro groom, Mike Fisher, she realized happily-ever-after was coming true. "When we put her tiara on, she looked at me and said, 'I'm getting married!'" recalled Melissa Schleicher, Underwood's makeup artist. "She's found the love of her life—Mike is her Prince Charming."

Fisher, 30, had to be something special to compete with the other steady in the singer's life, her 4-year-old rat terrier, Ace, who refused to give her up without a fight. As the couple sealed their vows with a kiss, guests seated beneath a tent at Georgia's Ritz-Carlton Reynolds Plantation, erupted into applause, while Ace (dressed in a pink tuxedo) simply erupted. "He was barking like mad," said Underwood, 27. He was jealous, said Fisher: "I took his woman!"

BEFORE THE BOOGIE

"It was a great party," said Underwood, who later donned a cocktail dress "to get my boogie on."

COUPLE ON THE CAKE

"My sister told me if I feel like tearing up, say the Pledge of Allegiance," Yearwood said of her efforts to keep her emotions in check. "I must have said it 20 times that night!"

Jason **MESNICK**
&
Molly **MALANEY**

Feb. 27, 2010
Rancho Palos Verdes, Calif.

Let Love Be Our Umbrella

IGNORING a torrential downpour, *The Bachelor*'s Jason Mesnick and Molly Malaney exchanged very soggy vows in front of 300 guests outside the Terranea Resort in Rancho Palos Verdes, Calif. "Jason was so sweet and wiped tears off Molly's face," said an onlooker. "They looked so happy to finally be married."

It had been a rocky road to the altar for the pair, who met when Malaney, 26, vied for the 34-year-old single dad's affection on *The Bachelor* last year. Mesnick first proposed to Melissa Rycroft but reunited with Malaney six weeks later, after dumping Rycroft on-air.

That drama seemed far behind as the bride—who wore a Monique Lhuillier gown and $600,000 in Neal Lane diamonds—sneaked away from their wedding guests (including *Bachelorette* alums Trista and Ryan Sutter), umbrella in hand. "Whenever they got a second alone, they would start kissing," said a source. "They looked extremely happy."

OFFICE ROMANCE

"She did cry after I cried," Krasinski told *Access Hollywood* about his emotional marriage proposal, "and we cried, and then everyone around us was crying."

Marriage, Italian Style

John KRASINSKI & Emily BLUNT

JULY 10, 2010
COMO, ITALY

He's from Massachusetts; she's from London. So the *Office* star, 31, and *The Devil Wears Prada* actress, 27, opted, natch, for a wedding weekend in Italy. Along with her Marchesa Bridal cream chiffon sweetheart draped gown, the bride, after the ceremony, wore a 3-carat Neil Lane round diamond. The party wasn't too shabby either: Pal George Clooney threw a candlelit dinner in the gardens of his Lake Como estate and, aboard a rented yacht, hosted a sunset cruise that included Bellinis, Prosecco, Meryl Streep and Matt Damon.

Transforming Experience

> ❝ THEY BOTH HAD THIS GIDDINESS . . . LIKE, 'I CAN'T BELIEVE YOU'RE MY HUSBAND!'"

Megan FOX
&
Brian AUSTIN GREEN

JUNE 24, 2010
KA`UPULEHU, HAWAII

t was a long buildup with a sudden, surprise and happy ending: Engaged for four years, *Transformers* star Megan Fox and *Beverly Hills, 90210* grad Brian Austin Green married with graceful flare, but little advance notice, on a Hawaiian beach, with only Green's 8-year-old son Kassius (with ex Vanessa Marcil), bearing witness. (They texted their parents the news that evening.) A local *kahuna-a* (Hawaiian priest) performed the ceremony; the couple exchanged rings, and Kassis donned a jade bracelet, blessed with seawater, to signify the three were now a family.

"They didn't need anything extravagant," said a source close to the couple. "Megan didn't want tons of flowers or diamonds. They just wanted it simple." As the Armani-clad bride, 24, walked barefoot down a sandy aisle to join Green, 37, on the beach at the Four Seasons in Ka`upulehu, it was clear they had accomplished that goal. "They were beyond happy," said the friend. "They decided a long time ago that they belonged with each other."

**Bride
of Borat**

Sacha Baron COHEN
&
Isla FISHER

MARCH 15, 2010
PARIS

GETTING HITCHED? "When you are in the public eye," actress Isla Fisher once said, "to keep that private and to make it happen without it being really visible is really very difficult." But she and fiancé of six years Sacha Baron Cohen, 39—"Borat" to much of the world—pulled it off, with just six guests at their hush-hush Paris wedding, a traditional Jewish ceremony. It was, said Fisher, "no fuss—just us!"

The couple, together eight years, have two children.

CARBO LOADING

Once a fitness trainer, Westling is now Duke of Västergötland.

Princess Victoria of SWEDEN
& Daniel WESTLING

JUNE 19, 2010
STOCKHOLM

Her father, King Carl XVI Gustaf, was said to be horrified when his oldest daughter first began dating a trainer she met at her gym eight years ago. But love won out, and Crown Princess Victoria, 33, and Daniel Westling, 37, said their "ja's" before a crowd of more than 1,200 guests (including Prince Albert of Monaco and Britain's Prince Edward) in Stockholm Cathedral.

"There are not enough superlatives," he recently said, "to describe her."

The wedding was a break with tradition, but perhaps a necessary one. A decade ago Victoria suffered from anorexia—in part, she said, because she felt that much of her life "was controlled by others." In marriage, she made her own happiness paramount. "The modern way is to marry someone you love," she once said, "not necessarily based on where he or she comes from."

DEEP DECOLLETAGE

Relax, traditionalists: "I'm definitely not going to get married in latex," said Perry, a fashion adventurer.

Katy PERRY
&
Russell BRAND

OCTOBER 23, 2010
RAJASTHAN, INDIA

"I WAS LIKE 25, 30 FEET AWAY FROM HIM," singer Katy Perry told *Esquire* about an early encounter with Brit comedian Russell Brand. "And I threw the bottle straight at him. Hit him smack dab on the head. Can you imagine the horrible feeling he had, when he was used to getting everything he wanted? I was like, 'You've met your match.'" Indeed. Could love be far behind? "I'm like, 'Oh, my God! I am you. You are me,'" Perry, who describes herself as "a [expletive] strong elephant of a woman," says of discoveries along the road to their 10-month engagement. "[We are] two divas in one house. . . . It's like splitting the atom: It shouldn't happen."

And then: fusion. In October the two were married in India, in a four-day affair that included a Bollywood party, a tiger safari and two elephants named Laxmi and Mala. "The very private and spiritual ceremony," said a statement from the couple's reps, ". . . was performed by a Christian minister and longtime friend of [Katy's] family. The backdrop was the inspirational and majestic countryside of northern India."

Miranda KERR
&
Orlando BLOOM

They kept it a secret

Australian-born Kerr has said that her "ideal situation" involves kids, a farm and a hammock.

Model Kerr, 27, and actor Bloom, 33, who had been dating almost three years, became engaged in June and wed a month later. Not long after that, a happy Kerr reported, "Yes, I am pregnant. Four months along." Said her mother, Therese: "They truly are gorgeous and very much in love and bring out the best in each other. . . . We are thrilled to welcome Orlando into the Kerr family."

The couple married in a gazebo overlooking the Pacific.

Ian ZIERING
&
Erin Kristine LUDWIG

MAY 28, 2010
NEWPORT COAST, CALIF.

GUYS, WRITE this down: "You're like a lit match in a dynamite factory." That, former *Beverly Hills, 90210* star Ian Ziering confessed, was his pickup line when he met nurse Erin Ludwig. Miraculously it worked: On May 28, in a zip code just an hour from Beverly Hills, Ziering, 46, and Ludwig, 25, married in a sunset ceremony at the Pelican Hill Resort. Cheering them on were Peach Pit pals Jason Priestley, Jennie Garth and Brian Austin Green. Ziering and Ludwig's romance was a whirlwind: Five months after they met, Ziering changed his Facebook status from "in a relationship" to "engaged," and it took only 12 more weeks to seal the deal.

Morissette and Souleye met in 2009.

Canadian Singer

Alanis MORISSETTE
&
Mario TREADWAY

MAY 22, 2010
LOS ANGELES

The wedding announcement came on Twitter. "So happy to share with you that my man Souleye and I got married," wrote Canadian singer Alanis Morissette, 36. "We're very excited to embark on this journey together." Souleye, 30, whose real name is Mario Treadway, is a rapper from Massachusetts; the two said their "I do's" in front of family in their Los Angeles home. The marriage was a first for both. (Morissette had previously been engaged to actor Ryan Reynolds; they broke up in 2007.)

Togetherness is not the only journey on which the couple will be embarking: In August, on Chelsea Handler's talk show, Morissette revealed that she was five months pregnant.

The Jonas Sister

IT WAS A great opening gambit: Determined to make his bride, Danielle Deleasa, feel like Cinderella on their wedding day, Kevin Jonas surprised her with a pre-ceremony gift: real glass slippers. "I couldn't believe it," said self-described "Jersey Girl" Danielle, 24. "The whole time I've dated Kevin, I never imagined this."

The fairy-tale vibe continued: As snow fell outside, the pair (she in Vera Wang Chantilly lace; he in a Brooks Brothers tux) married at a French-style château in Huntington, N.Y., in a tent decorated to resemble an enchanted forest. "When I saw her, I lost it," said Kevin, 23. "Once I lost it, it was like a tidal wave."

As for how this will affect life with his brothers, said Kevin: "Now they've got a sister, and I've got a wife. . . . I like the sound of that."

Kevin **JONAS**
&
Danielle **DELEASA**

DECEMBER 19, 2009
HUNTINGTON, N.Y.

WEDDINGS

Alicia KEYS
& Swizz BEATZ

JULY 31, 2010
CORSICA, FRANCE

Two months after announcing they were engaged and expecting, singer Alicia Keys, 30, and Swizz Beatz (real name Kasseem Dean), 32, were married by Deepak Chopra on the Mediterranean island of Corsica in front of family and friends, including Queen Latifa. The Grammy-magnet bride—she has 12—paired her Vera Wang gown with a more than 50-carat diamond halo headband (originally a necklace) by Jacob & Co.

Keys and Beatz were an item for about a year and half before announcing their engagement in June. He has two children from previous relationships; Keys, says a friend, is "thrilled to be a first-time mom. Said Chopra: "They are totally and completely and unabashedly in love."

HEART BEATZ

You may kiss the bride: Keys and Beatz celebrate in Corsica. Their son, Egypt Daoud Dean, was born in October.

A Ford in
Her Future

Harrison FORD
&
Calista FLOCKHART

JUNE 15, 2010
SANTA FE, N.MEX.

No invitations. No bridesmaids. No bouquet toss. He wore Wranglers, she a white sundress. Low-key and low-profile in the rest of their lives, Harrison Ford, 68, and Calista Flockhart, 46, a couple for more than eight years and engaged for one, married the same way—happily under the radar. The couple said their "I do's" at the Governor's Mansion in Sante Fe, N.Mex., where Ford was filming *Cowboys & Aliens*. "They are the most gracious and lovely couple," said Gov. Bill Richardson, who performed the simple, private ceremony. "They are obviously very much in love."

Rush LIMBAUGH
&
Kathryn ROGERS

JUNE 5, 2010
PALM BEACH

TOGETHER FOR SIX years, talk-radio host Rush Limbaugh, 59, and VIP liaison Kathryn Rogers, 34, wed before 400 guests at the Breakers Hotel. The marriage is Limbaugh's fourth. The party featured champagne, caviar and Sir Elton John. The singer's partner, David Furnish, said Elton was initially surprised by the offer, but "when it turned out to be a genuinely sincere invitation [to perform] . . . Elton said, 'Life is about building bridges, not walls.'"

WHITE WEDDING

"It's been 20 years that I would do all over again," Iglesias (with his family and staff) said of his life with Rijnsburger.

" 2010 MARKS 20 YEARS OF OUR LOVE"

Julio IGLESIAS

&

Miranda RIJNSBURGER

AUGUST 24, 2010
MARBELLA, SPAIN

One of Julio Iglesias' biggest hits is "To All the Girls I've Loved Before," but for a very long time there has been just one: Dutch model Miranda Rijnsburger, 45. The couple have been together for two decades and have five children. In August, with kids Miguel, Rodrigo, Guillermo and twins Cristina and Victoria standing by, Iglesias and Rijnsburger married in the tiny Virgen del Carmen church in Marbella, Spain. "They understood what the day meant and were very moved by it," said Iglesias, 67, of the private ceremony for their family. (His children by his first wife, daughter Chabeli and sons Julio Jr. and Enrique, did not attend.)

Just last March, Iglesias himself had marveled that he had somehow missed exchanging vows. "Sometimes I don't understand it," he said. "We've talked about a wedding five or six times. We've even made wedding plans before." Why now? "2010 marks 20 years of our love," he said. "It's the culmination of many years of unconditional support, a relationship that brought us five children who are our hearts."

IT'S OFFICIAL

The couple (signing their certificate) were married by three priests.

The newlyweds with their children (from bottom) Guillermo, 3, twins Victoria and Cristina, 9, Rodrigo, 11, and Miguel, 13.

Engagem

At L.A.'s SAG Awards in January.

Jane Krakowski & Robert Godley

"We're very much enjoying being engaged," said *30 Rock*'s Jane Krakowski, 42, who said yes to Robert Godley, a clothing designer, last winter. "We're still just looking. . . . I see that people got married in the Caribbean and people got married in Italy, and I'm like, 'Well, *those* all sound good!'"

CELEB COUPLES SAY "I WILL," THE FIRST STEP ON THE ROAD TO "I DO"

ents

America Ferrera & Ryan Piers Williams

Big changes for America: Weeks after *Ugly Betty* ended, reps for star America Ferrera confirmed she was engaged to Ryan Piers Williams. They met when he cast her in a student film at USC.

Valerie Bertinelli & Tom Vitale

Actress and weight-loss icon Valerie Bertinelli, 50, and Tom Vitale, 49, planned a fall wedding. "I've never felt more beautiful at any weight," she says, "than when Tom looks at me."

Zoë Saldana & Keith Britton

Something old, something new, something borrowed, someone blue? Zoë Saldana, 32, who played *Avatar*'s azure heroine, will wed beau Keith Britton, who runs a fashion website.

Prince Albert & Charlene Wittstock

After a *loooooooong* bachelorhood, Monaco's Prince Albert II, 52, announced he'll take the plunge with former Olympic swimmer Charlene Wittstock, 32, a South African. "Charlene has quietly learned how everything works," said a friend. "It's as if she has been apprenticing."

Wittstock stood by the prince through revelations he had fathered children out of wedlock. Said a friend of Albert's: "He really loves her."

"I've been in love with him since not long after we met," says Lambert (with Shelton at the '09 CMA awards).

Miranda Lambert & Blake Shelton

For a country-star couple whose idea of romance is shopping for bow-and-arrow sets, the Oklahoma woods were the perfect place for a proposal. "I was wearing a camo jacket and no makeup," says Miranda Lambert, 27, of the moment Blake Shelton asked for her hand. "It was very country, perfectly redneck and totally us."

Christina Applegate & Martyn Lenoble

Samantha Who? star Cristina Applegate and her beau of two years, Dutch musician Martyn Lenoble, 41, became engaged on Valentine's Day. It will be the second marriage for both. In July, the actress, who had a double mastectomy en route to beating breast cancer in 2009, announced that she was expecting a child. Said a thrilled Applegate, 39: "It's not about you anymore."

Applegate and Lenoble in L.A. last August.

'N Sync
Dad

Joey & Kelly
FATONE

KLOEY FATONE
JANUARY 11, 2010

Babies

THEY'RE HERE, THEY'RE CUTE, AND THEIR PARENTS ARE TICKLED PINK (AND BLUE)

When, five months into her pregnancy, Joey Fatone's wife, Kelly, 34, was diagnosed with a genetic disorder that led to chronic fatigue, doctors put her on strict bed rest, leaving dad to care for both her and daughter Briahna, 9. "I'd drive her to school and come home and take care of Kelly," he recalls. "It was really tough on all of us." The happy ending came when Kelly delivered a healthy little girl, Kloey, on Jan. 11—although a tape Joey made during delivery may have to be edited. "Suddenly Kelly starts swearing because the epidural didn't work," he says. "We're going to have some explaining to do someday when Kloey watches the tape." The Fatones say their family is now complete. "I'm outnumbered—surrounded by girls," says Joey, 33, "but I wouldn't have it any other way."

Michelle & Jim Bob
DUGGAR

JOSIE DUGGAR
DECEMBER 10, 2009

With 19 kids, Michelle Duggar does the best she can to give individual time to each, seeking out private moments during shopping trips, homework or, with the older kids, very late at night. "I can sleep later," says Michelle. "This is important now."

Life became even more complicated for Michelle, 44, and her husband, Jim Bob Duggar, 45, who star in the TLC reality show *19 Kids and Counting*, when their newest addition, Josie, was born three months premature, with medical issues that required constant monitoring. "That was the scariest part," says Michelle of Josie's arrival in the Duggar's Tontitown, Ark., home. "I had never dealt with monitors, oxygen tanks and tubes, any of that." The logistics were daunting: When 11 of her children came down with chicken pox, Michelle and Josie, whose immune system was still fragile, stayed elsewhere.

The Duggars had received a fair amount of criticism from people who think 19 children is too many. "We don't expect people to understand," says Jim Bob, a devout Baptist who views each child as a gift from God. "We are following our convictions."

First-Time Mom

TIFFANI THIESSEN had her birth plan all worked out: She would stay calm using self-hypnosis through labor, then immediately breast-feed her newborn daughter as soon as it was over.

Things didn't exactly go according to plan. "First my water didn't break; they had to do it for me," says the actress, 36. "Then the baby wasn't descending because the cord was wrapped around her neck." After 30 hours of labor, she had a C-section. "Once she was finally out, I didn't even get to hold her before they whisked her away. You're staring across the room, like, 'Hello? Over here!' The whole thing was very surreal."

Since bringing daughter Harper Renn Smith home, however, things have been far less chaotic. "She sleeps anywhere from three to four hours at a time at night, which is not bad," says Thiessen, whose husband, actor Brady Smith, 39, gets up with her to pitch in on nighttime duty. "She's got these chubby cheeks like her mother," says Thiessen, "but she looks like both of us."

And caring for a newborn? "It's a lot of work," says Thiessen. Not that she minds: "This is a kind of love that you never really knew about. You haven't known this person for very long, but you love them so much."

Tiffani
THIESSEN
&
Brady SMITH

HARPER RENN SMITH
JUNE 15, 2010

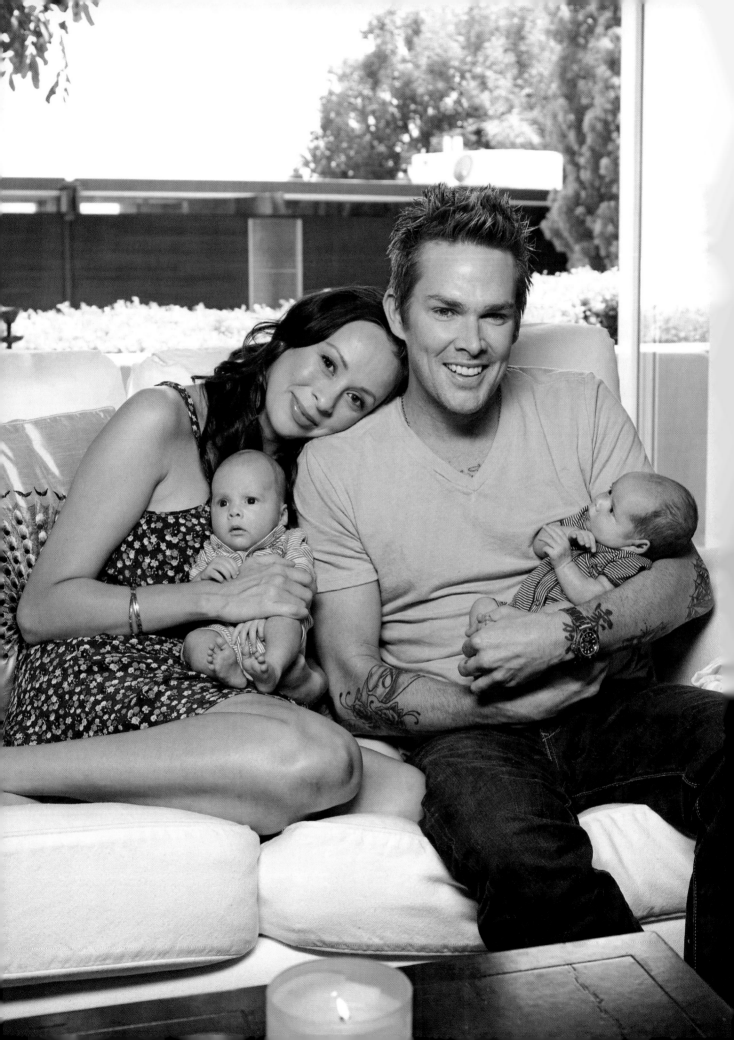

Krishna, said the *Top Chef* host, is "a big eater."

Rockin' Daddy

Mark
McGRATH
&
Carin KINGSLAND

HARTLEY GRACE AND LYDON EDWARD
APRIL 29, 2010

Since becoming a dad in April, Sugar Ray singer Mark McGrath has added to his vocabulary. "I'd never used the word 'cute' in 42 years," says the tattooed rocker. "Now I say it 10 times a day!" And with good reason—two, actually: son Lydon Edward and daughter Hartley Grace. Parenthood has been an adjustment for McGrath and fiancée Carin Kingsland, 38, his on-off partner of 16 years. "Our dates used to involve booze and fun, and now it's bottles and onesies," says McGrath. "We go to Target at 8 a.m. to beat the crowds! And we couldn't be happier."

Getting there wasn't easy. Initially reluctant to settle down, McGrath realized the clock was ticking for Kingsland, who faced additional obstacles to getting pregnant: She had lost one ovary to a benign tumor and had fibroids and cysts. So when they didn't conceive after more than a year of trying the old-fashioned way, McGrath dipped into savings for one $15,000 round of IVF. When it worked, says Kingsland, "we were shocked. But I always had faith." Now they're marveling at being a family of four. Lydon is "impatient and knows what he wants," like his dad, says Kingsland, while Hartley is "calm and sweet like her mother," says McGrath. "Changing diapers, seeing them smile—it's like hearing your song on the radio for the first time," he says. "Nothing has meant more to me than these two children."

Padma
LAKSHMI
&
Adam DELL

KRISHNA THEA LAKSHMI
FEBRUARY 20, 2010

YOUR HEART just explodes with love," said Padma Lakshmi of the moment daughter Krishna was placed in her arms. "It's a burst of joy."

Enough, apparently, to overcome a bit of drama. Lakshmi, 40, announced her pregnancy in 2009 and didn't reveal the baby's father. He turned out to be her ex, Adam Dell, 40, a venture capitalist. A disagreement about how much time he could spend with Krishna became public, and Lakshmi sought to keep it under wraps. "I have a newborn!" she said. "I just want some peace and privacy."

Real Housewife

Bethenny FRANKEL
&
Jason HOPPY

BRYN CASEY HOPPY
MAY 8, 2010

Everything that's happened is exciting, but it's nothing like having her in your arms," says Bethenny Frankel of newborn Bryn. "I live for this baby." The star of *Real Housewives of New York City* and, later, her own show, *Bethenny Getting Married?*, Frankel, 40, revealed in July that her own upbringing had been a mess. "I never had a true childhood," she says. "There was a lot of destruction: alcohol abuse, eating disorders and violent fights." Her mother, she says, "was extremely volatile"; her dad, a famous horse trainer who walked out when she was 4, "lived a very hotshot life. It wasn't a life for a little girl. I was always at restaurants or the track." Thus experienced, Frankel vows to do better: "I just want to give her the life I didn't have."

Frankel and sales exec Jason Hoppy, 39, wed March 28, 2010.

Splits

IN A YEAR OF BIG BUST-UPS, SUSAN SARANDON AND TIM ROBBINS, HALLE BERRY AND GABRIEL AUBRY AND AL AND TIPPER GORE CALL IT QUITS

Longtime Couple

Susan SARANDON & Tim ROBBINS

They represented a rare breed: the Hollywood couple that stays together. Having long ago silenced the doubters, the better-with-age older woman and the boyishly handsome younger man seemed made for each other, sharing movie projects, political causes and child-rearing—one of hers, two of theirs—for 23 years, since meeting on the set of the 1988 baseball film *Bull Durham*. As Susan Sarandon once told *Ladies Home Journal*, "I believe in one-stop shopping."

It was a stunner, then, when the Oscar-winning duo announced their split two days before Christmas 2009. Rumors swirled that Sarandon, 64, had fallen for Jonathan Bricklin, 33, whose Manhattan table-tennis club counts her as an investor. The pair denied it.

A friend of Tim Robbins, 52, said there had long been trouble under the surface. "Every time I heard Tim talking about their [relationship], he said, 'Susan and I are having problems.'" Even so, added an insider, "they raised three amazing kids together. Obviously they did something right."

BETTER DAYS

The couple (in 2004) were together 23 years but never wed. "I had forgotten we didn't," Sarandon once joked. "There was so much children and real estate."

**Model
Separation**

Halle BERRY
&
Gabriel AUBRY

Halle Berry and Gabriel Aubry looked the happy couple on a trip to the Los Angeles Zoo on April 2 with their daughter, Nahla, 2, but the togetherness was for show: Days later it became public that the couple had split up months ago. Although some reports said Aubry, 35—a French-Canadian model Berry, 44, met at a Versace shoot in 2005—initiated the split, a source close to both said no way: "She kicked him out ... because he wasn't able to pull his weight in the relationship, and she wanted to move on. She just realized she was growing beyond the relationship and thought it best to end things."

For Nahla's sake, the two continued to spend time together. "They're going to co-parent and go on with their lives," said a friend of Berry's. "They will be in each other's lives forever."

Melissa ETHERIDGE

Tammy Lynn MICHAELS

SINGER Melissa Etheridge told Oprah that her split from partner Tammy Lynn Michaels was "as mutual as those things can be." Then things go ugly, fast. "Stop telling the press it was mutual," Michaels wrote on her blog, claiming that she was "blindsided" when Etheridge, 49, filed for divorce. For her part, Etheridge complained that when she went to visit the couple's 4-year-old twins, Johnnie Rose and Miller, she was served with court papers instead. The two are battling over custody.

Michaels (right) wrote that Etheridge's new CD sounded like a "breakup album."

"What they had was profound and real," said a friend. "It just wasn't permanent."

End of a Fine Romance

Jenny McCARTHY & Jim CARREY

They had been a fixture for five years, so Jim Carrey and Jenny McCarthy's decision to split caught even close friends off guard. "It was a huge surprise even to those of us who are close to them," said a source. "Everyone around them is sad." Still, friends say there had always been an underlying tension between the bubbly, outgoing McCarthy and Carrey, whose manic comedy masks a darker, more withdrawn side. "Jim can run hot and he can run cold," said a source close to the couple. "He is someone who desperately needs to be with someone, then just as desperately needs to be alone. But at the same time, he can be a very loving, very compassionate guy."

In separate statements, Carrey, 48, and McCarthy, 38, characterized the breakup as amicable. Noting that she "will always keep Jim as a leading man in my heart," McCarthy—whose autistic son Evan, 8, has an exceptionally tight bond with Carrey—said also that she would remain close to Carrey's daughter Jane, 23. For his part, Carrey tweeted, "I'm grateful 4 the many blessings we've shared."

SEPARATED

"This was not an overnight thing," a friend said of the couple (in L.A. on June 1).

"They have a child together, so they're going to do what's best," said a friend.

Courteney COX

& David ARQUETTE

AFTER SHOOTING *Scream 4* scenes together in Michigan last summer, Courteney Cox and David Arquette would retire to separate trailers. "It seemed like the worst-kept secret that things were weird between them," said an on-set source.

There were other hints. In June Arquette told PEOPLE, "Relationships take a lot of work." In August Cox told IN STYLE, "You should realize that the intriguing things you fall in love with will probably become the things you don't like."

On Oct. 11, Cox, 46, and Arquette, 39, announced that, after 11 years of marriage, they were on a "trial separation."

A wobbly sounding Arquette went on the Howard Stern radio show the next morning to offer his own candid take on events. In June, he said, "she [told] me, 'I don't wanna be your mother anymore.' I respected that. I've been going to therapy. I'm trying to grow up . . . trying to figure out myself and my world, and so is she." He said that he and Cox had not slept together for months before their split, then publicly apologized the next day for over-sharing.

The future? "It's tough," said a friend of the couple's, who have a daughter, Coco, 6. "Honestly, only time will tell."

Christina AGUILERA

& Jordan BRATMAN

Christina Aguilera and her husband, producer Jordan Bratman, were sipping champagne aboard a yacht off the Italian coast, and they looked miserable. "They were in the most beautiful place in the world and having the worst time," a close friend of the couple's told PEOPLE. "That was the wake-up call." Soon after, Bratman, 33, moved out of the couple's Beverly Hills home, and on Oct. 14 Aguilera filed for divorce.

Rumblings of trouble started when Aguilera—who wed Bratman in an estimated $2 million ceremony in Napa Valley, Calif. in 2005—was spotted without her wedding ring in March. A source close to the singer says that during an earlier separation, while filming the upcoming movie *Burlesque*, she strayed. "What kept them together so long," said a friend, "is [their 2-year-old son] Max."

"It's not easy, and there have been a lot of tears and sadness," Aguilera, 29, told *Redbook* of the split. "It's impossible to redefine yourself and your life overnight."

The Breaking Point

John & Elizabeth
EDWARDS

As recently as May '09, Elizabeth (with John in '08) wrote in her memoir, *Resilience*, "I am his and he is mine."

A three-year saga of lying and betrayal reached a dénouement of sorts when Elizabeth Edwards, 61, separated from former Senator, and presidential wannabe, John Edwards, 57, her husband of 32 years. During the 2008 presidential campaign, John Edwards had an affair with, and impregnated, his campaign "videographer," Rielle Hunter, 46, while Elizabeth was battling terminal cancer. On Jan. 21, after repeated denials, he admitted paternity of his child with Hunter ("I am Quinn's father"). A few weeks earlier, Elizabeth had called it quits. "She said, 'I've had it. I can't do this. I want my life back,'" said her sister Nancy Anania.

Later, Hunter, in an interview in *GQ*, said that she and John had been ensnared in a "force field" of love that would last "till death do us part." His friends dismissed that claim, with one calling it "total fantasy." For Elizabeth that brouhaha was "a little bump in the road," said her sister. "She's working at creating a new life."

Al & Tipper
GORE

WHEN THE GORES announced in a June 1 e-mail—two weeks after their 40th anniversary—that after "long and careful consideration" they were separating, stunned friends were left scrambling for explanations. The best guess: diverging passions. Tipper, 62, "always wanted to be a normal person and have fun," said a longtime associate. Al, 62, who juggles environmental and business positions, perhaps "never learned to relax." Still, said a friend, "these two will remain the best of friends. They've been friends for life."

SPLIT DECISION

PDAs past: The couple (in 2008) once made out at a Democratic Convention.

Sam MENDES
&
Kate WINSLET

Nothing seemed amiss when Kate Winslet walked down the red carpet at the Academy Awards. "The pressure is certainly off," said the actress, who won last year's Best Actress award. "It's really nice just to be able to relax and enjoy it."

The evening itself, it seems, may have been a bit of a performance: A week later Winslet, 34, and her husband, director Sam Mendes, 44, announced they had quietly separated weeks earlier. After almost seven years of marriage and a son together, Joe, 7 (Winslet also has a daughter, Mia, 10, from an earlier marriage), the split "is entirely amicable and is by mutual agreement," their attorneys said in a statement. "Both parties are fully committed to the future joint parenting of their children."

"It's really sad; they just grew apart," said someone who had worked with both of them. "It's tough to be married in this business."

FAREWELL,
VIENNA

During the nicey-
nicey phase, Vienna
said things like,
"He notices when I
change my toenail
polish colors!"

Jake
PAVELKA

&

Vienna GIRARDI

He was a handsome 32-year-old pilot and season 14's prize on *The Bachelor*; she was a 24-year-old former Hooters waitress who's alienated most of her rivals on the show, as well as legions of viewers. But when Jake Pavelka picked Vienna Girardi to be his much-publicized fiancée, he passionately defended his choice, and their love, to a skeptical world. "I can't wait for everyone to see the Vienna I fell in love with," he said. "I'm absolutely in love. I'm soaring!"

Mayday! Mayday! Bail out! Three months later the couple crashed, spectacularly. A former classmate of Girardi's said the two were just different people ("Her idea of fun . . . is getting crazy and having a good time; he's more like . . . "Let's play Yahtzee!'"). Pavelka was far more pointed, accusing Girardi of being lazy, a sponge, jealous of his success, two-timing and, most shocking, selling a story about their romance, behind his back, to a tabloid (Girardi had no comment). "I absolutely feel betrayed," said the once-again eligible bachelor, who broke up with Girardi by phone. "I feel like I don't even know her."

Kelsey GRAMMER
&
Camille DONATACCI

"Camille and I shared many wonderful things throughout our years together; there were just a few things that we couldn't work out," said Kelsey Grammer, 55, after his wife of 13 years, Camille Donatacci Grammer (above), 42, filed for divorce in July. One of the things it seems they could not work out: As the actor's rep confirmed one month later, Grammer has a new girlfriend, Kayte Walsh, 29, who is pregnant with his child.

BRIEFLY
NOTED

You don't have to be married for a split to set gossip sites atwitter. Two noted uncouples:

Joe Jonas and
Demi Lovato

"We've been best friends for a long time," said Joe Jonas of going public, in March, with his *Camp Rock* costar. "Now we're just kind of taking the next step." In May they split—but still toured together. Lovato later quit the tour and sought treatment for "emotional and physical issues."

Taylor Swift and
Taylor Lautner

Fans of same-name couples rooted passionately for the two Taylors—T2, anyone?—who met while filming *Valentine's Day*, but their romance was brief. Some Swift fans thought her song "Back to December," containing the line, "I'm sorry for that night," alluded to their breakup.

Never the Twain shall meet? No way! Shania and Thiébaud were all smiles at the Red Cross Ball.

Twain Back on Track

Mutt LANGE
&
Shania TWAIN

Two years after Shania Twain, 45, discovered her husband, Mutt Lange, 62, was having an affair with her best friend, Marie-Anne Thiébaud, a Swiss court declared the couple divorced. Although legally single, Twain was anything but on the market: After the affair was discovered she and Frédéric Thiébaud, 40, Marie-Anne's ex, found solace in each other's company, then something much more. Last year Twain hinted at their burgeoning romance on her website; this year a radiant Twain and the handsome Thiébaud went public together at the Swiss Red Cross Ball in Geneva. "Her happiness certainly shone through," said a Red Cross official. "They are a great addition to each other's lives."

Twain (with Lange in 2003) is now Mutt-free.

Bob GUINEY
&
Rebecca BUDIG

EVERY relationship has issues, and you can either work through them or you can't," says Rebecca Budig. "Ultimately we couldn't."

At that point, though, the surprise wasn't the split, but its aftermath: Despite filing for divorce in April after six years of marriage, the *All My Children* actress has remained on congenial terms with her ex, "Bachelor Bob" Guiney, the star of *The Bachelor*'s fourth season. Their secret? "A lot of therapy," says Guiney, 39, along with "our love and care for one another. I truly want her to be happy, and I know without a doubt that she wants the same for me."

To the point that when Budig, 37, found herself with a "very special" new man in her life, she couldn't wait to relay the news to her ex. "Bob was, like, 'Are we really *having* this conversation?'" she recalls, laughing. But all was cool. Says Budig: "We really honor the commitment we made to each other."

" I WILL ALWAYS LOVE BOB. WE WILL ALWAYS BE THERE FOR EACH OTHER"

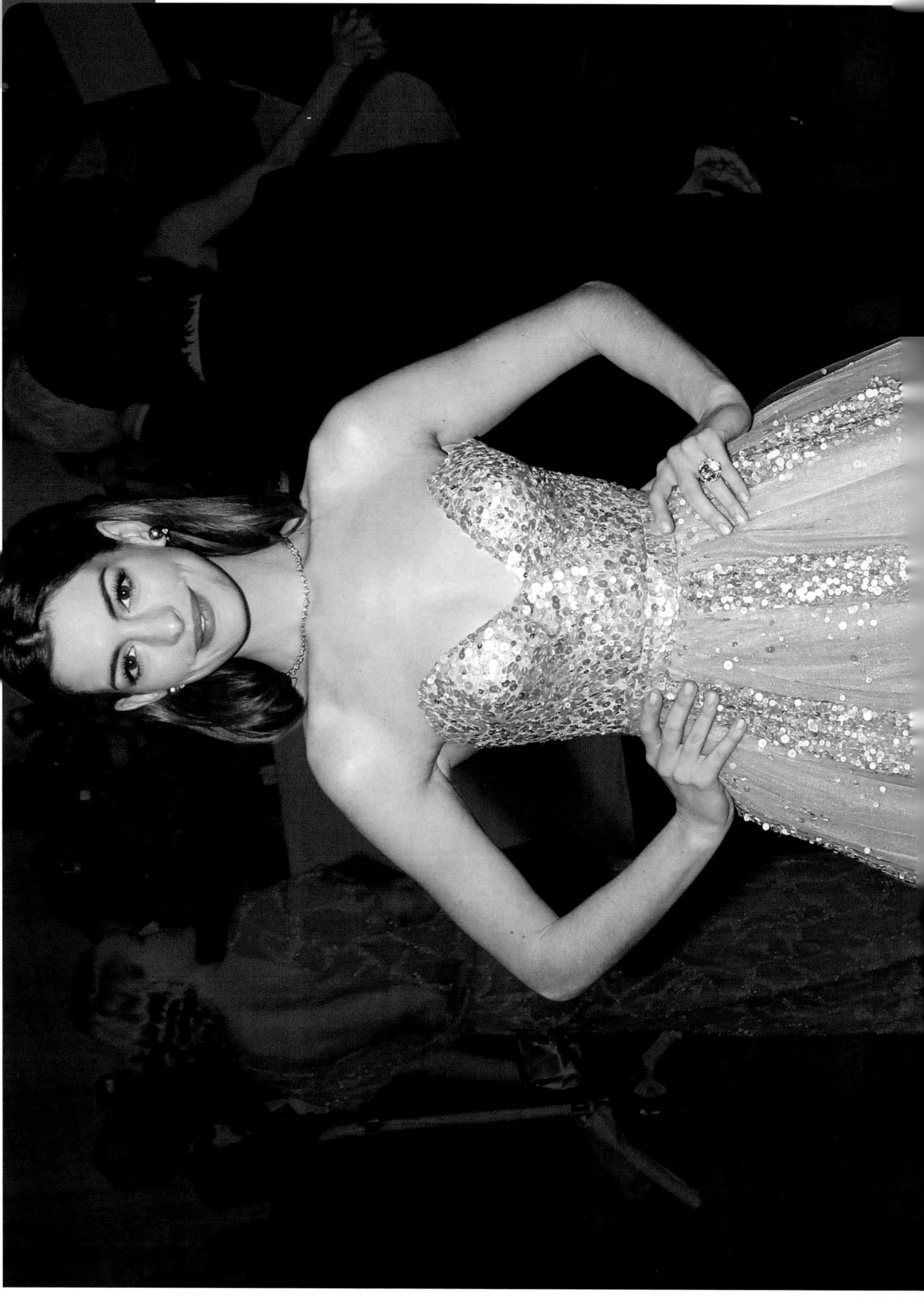

Best in Show

STARS BROUGHT THEIR GLAM GAME—AND ANNE HATHAWAY A BIT OF CINDERELLA SPARKLE—TO THE OSCARS, GOLDEN GLOBES, EMMYS AND OTHER RED-CARPET VENUES

OSCARS

MARCH 7, 2010 LOS ANGELES

Cameron DIAZ — OSCAR DE LA RENTA

Vera FARMIGA — MARCHESA

Sandra BULLOCK — MARCHESA

Kate WINSLET
YVES SAINT LAURENT

Penélope CRUZ
DANA KARAN COUTURE

Kristen STEWART
MONIQUE LHUILLIER

Zoe SALDANA
GIVENCHY BY RICCARDO TISCI

GOLDEN GLOBES

Jan. 17, 2010 Los Angeles

Emily
BLUNT
DOLCE & GABBANA

Jennifer
ANISTON
VALENTINO

Kate
HUDSON
MARCHESA

Cameron
DIAZ

Christina
AGUILERA

Marion
COTILLARD

ALEXANDER McQUEEN

VERSACE

CHRISTIAN DIOR

Diane
KRUGER

CHRISTIAN LACROIX
HAUTE COUTURE

GRAMMYS

JAN. 31, 2010 LOS ANGELES

Beyoncé KNOWLES
STEPHANE ROLLAND

Taylor SWIFT
KAUFMANFRANCO

Lea MICHELE
ROMONA KEVEZA

AWARD

Heidi
KLUM
EMILIO PUCCI

Mary J.
BLIGE
GUCCI

Jennifer
LOPEZ
VERSACE

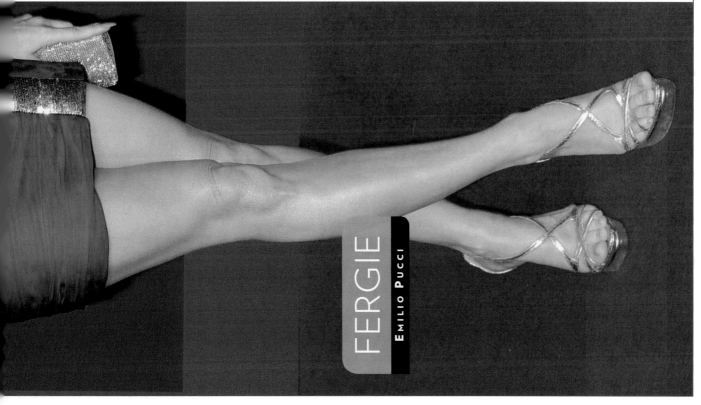

FERGIE
EMILIO PUCCI

BEST *of the* REST

Jennifer ANISTON
DRESS: **VALENTINO**
JACKET: **ALEXANDER McQUEEN**
Bounty Hunter Premiere, London

Carey MULLIGAN
CHRISTOPHER KANE
RESORT 2011
Toronto Film Festival

Lea MICHELE
CATHERINE MALANDRINO
Screen Actors Guild Awards

Naomi **WATTS**
Stella McCartney
Costume Institute Gala,
New York

Emily **BLUNT**
Dior
Emmy Awards

Angelina **JOLIE**
Emporio Armani
Salt Premiere,
Los Angeles

Eva **LONGORIA**
Emilio Pucci
Cannes Film Festival

WORST DRESSED

Ke$ha

Making $$$$, $aving on $tyle.

Kelis

One part Statue of Liberty, two parts ringmaster.

Shauna SANDS

Not so much worst dressed as ... undressed?

Kelly ROWLAND
Zen question: Can too little have too much? Discuss!

Kat VON D
Just keep staring—a picture will emerge!

Björk
Fact: In winter Icelanders keep flowers alive by wearing them.

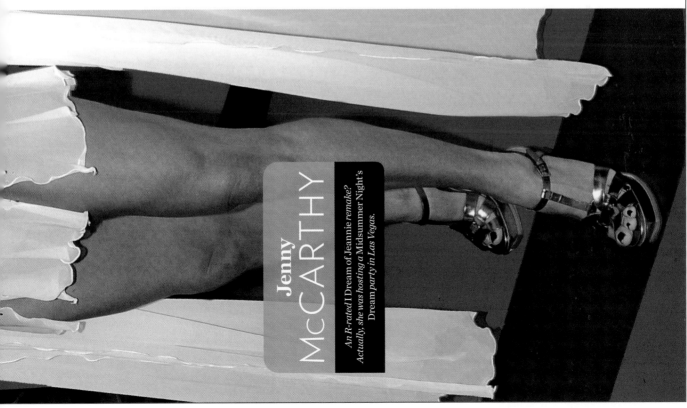

Jenny McCARTHY
An R-rated I Dream of Jeannie remake? Actually, she was hosting a Midsummer Night's Dream party in Las Vegas.

Farewell

SAYING GOODBYE TO HOLLYWOOD LEGENDS, BABY BOOMER HEROES, TROUBLED CHILD STARS AND THE RECLUSIVE AUTHOR WHO GAVE US HOLDEN CAULFIELD

Diff'rent Strokes Star

Gary COLEMAN

1968-2010
PROVO, UTAH

He was given up for adoption at 1 day old and starred in a TV hit, *Diff'rent Strokes*, at age 10. When that ended, Gary Coleman embarked on the familiar and depressing journey of many former child stars, made worse by medical problems—kidney failure as a child lead to his diminutive stature—and financial trouble. "I have four strikes against me," he said in 1999. "I'm black, I'm short, I'm intelligent, and I have a medical condition." He took odd jobs—including, famously, a stint as a mall cop—behaved badly and was mocked by comics.

Even after he died in Utah following a brain hemorrhage, the sad show continued as an ex-wife and ex-girlfriend battled over what little was left of his millions. His Rosebud, it seems, was model trains: Coleman had an enormous collection and sometimes worked in a Culver City hobby shop. "That was his big escape," said Allied Model Trains' Fred Hill. "The customers loved him, and he loved the attention."

PRIME-TIME PRECOCITY

After *Diff'rent Strokes* ended, Coleman (above, with Shavar Ross) "found himself out in the cold," said his former agent. "A lot of bitterness in his life came from that."

TOP OF THE WORLD

"People were just drawn to him," said Gary's mother, Sue Coleman.

HIS RENEGADE runway shows—with models walking through fiery hoops or presented as asylum patients—produced shock and awe. But his final act simply broke hearts: On Feb. 11 McQueen, 40, hanged himself in his London apartment. Friends blamed the cumulative effect of the suicide of his mentor, Isabella Blow, in 2007, and the death of his beloved mother, Joyce, nine days before his own. "[B]een a f------ awful week but my friends have been great," he tweeted on Feb. 7, "but now I have to somehow pull myself together."

Sadly, he couldn't. "His independence, his skill, his quiet fortitude," said Sarah Jessica Parker, "will be an unthinkable loss."

Punk Guru

Malcolm McLAREN

1946–2010

BELLINZONA, SWITZERLAND

t's better to be a flamboyant failure," Malcolm McLaren once said, "than a benign success." Spoken like a true godfather of Punk—which McLaren might as well have had printed on his business card. An anarchic but media-savvy promoter, he once owned a design boutique with then-partner Vivenne Westwood and later brought the Sex Pistols into the world. Follow-up projects were no less experimental, if easier on the ears. "Above all else he was an entertainer," former Sex Pistol John Lydon said of his friend, who died of mesothelioma at 64, "and I will miss him, and so should you."

BELOVED BAD BOY

The Queen made McQueen (at a '09 show) a Commander of the Order of the British Empire in 2003.

Alexander
McQUEEN

1969-2010
LONDON

" SHE WAS
LIKE NO
OTHER,
A BRIGHT
LIGHT …"
—KATHY NAJIMY

Brittany MURPHY

1977-2009

LOS ANGELES

Months later there are still more questions than answers. On Dec. 20, 2009, Brittany Murphy, 32, who broke through in *Clueless* and played Eminem's girlfriend in *8 Mile*, was found dead in her Hollywood Hills home. The actress's thin frame and party-girl past led to speculation that illegal drugs may have played a role. But the coroner's report, released over two months later, told a simpler story: Murphy, who had been suffering flu-like symptoms, died of pneumonia, with prescription drugs—including the painkiller Vicoprofen and the antidepressant Fluoxetine, which she was reportedly taking for severe menstrual cramps—and anemia as contributing factors. Her husband, British screenwriter Simon Monjack, 40, said that they had no idea she was so sick. "I am feeling beyond devastated," he said.

But the story didn't end there. Monjack, a mysterious character who had a history of financial problems, was accused by Murphy's former business manager of draining her accounts of hundreds of thousands of dollars in the weeks after her death. His mother, Linda, was accused of trying to toss Murphy's mother, Sharon, who had lived with her daughter, out of the house (Linda denied any wrongdoing).

Then, on May 23, the saga took another bizarre and tragic twist: Simon Monjack was found dead in the same bedroom in which his wife had died. Although he had prescription drugs in his system, they weren't at lethal levels: Like Brittany, the coroner determined, he died of pneumonia.

Murphy and Monjack: a marriage with many mysteries.

SMOOTH OPERATORS

"Pee Wee Reese stood up for Jackie Robinson, and Bob stood up for me," Bill Cosby said of his *I Spy* costar.

Robert CULP

1930-2010
LOS ANGELES

n 1965, Robert Culp was cast in *I Spy*, a caper series about two secret agents disguised as traveling tennis pros, with the not yet hugely famous comic Bill Cosby, making them the first black-white leading costars in TV history. "We were an integrated team," said Cosby, who also recalled that Culp showed him the acting ropes: "He had to teach me how to open a door properly." And when Cosby won the first of three Emmys for the part—Culp never won—"Bob said, 'I'm proud of you.'"

The response was typical of Culp, who projected a "cool, hipster exterior," says actress Patricia Heaton. When he'd arrive on the *Everybody Loves Raymond* set for his recurring role as her father, "he wore this Playboy Mansion letter jacket, like a varsity jacket!" The five-times married actor was, in fact, a fixture at the manse, even, said close pal Hugh Hefner, coining its unofficial motto: "Gentlemen, gentlemen, be of good cheer, for they are out there, and we are in here!"

But Culp also had a serious side, notably campaigning for civil rights. "He would hook into something that spoke to his heart," said his son, actor Joseph Culp, 47. "He had a strong sense of what's right." And, said Cosby, Culp, who died of a heart attack at 79 while walking near his L.A. home, was a constant in a changeable town. Each time they'd reunite, said his former partner, "even if it was after five years, it was like he'd just gone across the street for a loaf of bread."

John FORSYTHE

1918-2010
SANTA YNEZ, CALIF.

THE VOICE and the look: It was a one-two punch. In the '30s he announced Dodgers baseball; by the '50s John Forsythe was the bemused paterfamilias on the sitcom *Bachelor Father*. Next, as the voice of Charlie on *Charlie's Angels*, he was heard but never seen; by the '80s he was the dashing éminence grise on *Dynasty*. Ever modest, Forsythe once called himself "a vastly usable, not wildly talented actor." Friends new better. "He was a gifted actor," said Heather Locklear, "who knew the true meaning of being gracious and kind."

A hipster who hung with Hef.

"WE RODE THE HIGHWAYS OF AMERICA AND CHANGED THE WAY MOVIES WERE MADE"
—PETER FONDA

Dennis
HOPPER

1936-2010
VENICE, CALIF.

I'M NOT REALLY A person who looks back on my life," Dennis Hopper said in 2009. "It was really a wonderful time. No, I don't think I'd change a thing."

It was, indeed, quite a ride. He first gained notice in *Rebel Without a Cause* and was impressed with the film's star. "I believed I was the best actor I knew my age," Hopper said. "That is, until I saw James Dean." In 1969 he directed and starred in *Easy Rider,* a saga about drug-dealing bikers that became a counterculture touchstone. Said costar and friend Jack Nicholson: "Dennis stands out because of his edge, his sincerity, the honesty he conveys."

Also, perhaps, for his appetites: By the late '70s, Hopper, by his own estimate, was putting away a case of beer, half a gallon of rum and three grams of coke per day. "What can I tell you?," he told PEOPLE years later after cleaning up. "I was a fun guy."

Free-spirited too: Hopper married five times and had four children. Not surprisingly, the drama continued even after his death, at 74, from prostate cancer. The actor had been locked in a bitter divorce battle with his fifth wife, Victoria Duffy Hopper, 43; a prenup called for her to inherit 25 percent of his estate if they we're still married and living together at his death. She is currently living in a guest house on his property with their daughter Galen, 7; Victoria and Hopper's adult children will meet in probate court.

Theater Royalty

Lynn REDGRAVE

1943-2010
KENT, CONN.

Onstage and off, she radiated pluck—never more so than in the 1966 film *Georgy Girl,* which earned her an Oscar nomination at 23. A prominent member of an acting dynasty—her parents were West End legends Sir Michael Redgrave and Rachel Kempson; her siblings Vanessa and the late Corin Redgrave; her nieces Joely and the late Natasha Richardson—Lynn Redgrave starred in the '80s sitcom *House Calls* and was nominated for three Tonys and another Oscar, in 1998, for *Gods and Monsters.* In love with acting, she even sought solace in performing after being stricken with breast cancer in 2003. "She said Dr. Theater got her though the hard times," said a friend. "She was always positive like that."

"She was always looking to disappear inside a character," said a director.

Baby Boom
Icon

Fess
PARKER

1924-2010
Los Olivos, Calif.

BORN ON A mountain top in Tennessee/ Kilt him a b'ar when he was only 3 . . .": If you know that song—and every baby-boom boy of a certain age does—or ever owned a coonskin cap, you have Fess Parker to thank. As an actor, the 6'6" native Texan scored a sort of frontier daily double, starring first as Davy Crockett for Disney and, later, for six seasons on TV as Daniel Boone. But there was more to Parker than a fringe jacket and a flintlock: After leaving Hollywood, he opened successful inns and a winery in California.

Neal costarred with Gary Cooper in *The Fountainhead* (1949).

Peter GRAVES

1926-2010
LOS ANGELES

HIS SILVER-HAIRED gravitas suited his *Mission Impossible* role, but offscreen Graves, wed to wife Joan for 60 years, was a devoted husband and dad. "He personified something midwestern," said *MI* costar Barbara Bain. "He was a man, not a boy."

Screen Legend

Patricia NEAL

1926-2010
EDGARTOWN, MASS.

She lived a stupifyingly dramatic life. Patricia Neal appeared in over 30 movies, including *The Subject Was Roses* and *Breakfast at Tiffany's*, and won and Oscar for *Hud*. Offscreen, she had an affair with Gary Cooper and was devastated after it ended. Later she married writer Roald Dahl and, while pregnant, suffered three strokes; Dahl helped her relearn to walk and talk. (Sadly, they divorced in 1983, after Dahl had an affair with her close friend.) The actress, who grew up in Knoxville, summed up her remarkable resilience in her autobiography, *As I Am*: "We Tennessee hillbillies don't conk that easy, so I stayed alive."

Pernell ROBERTS

1930-2010
MALIBU, CALIF.

Restless Cowboy

HE COSTARRED FOR SIX seasons on *Bonanza* but really, *really* wanted out. "I feel I am an aristocrat in my field," he said. "My being part of *Bonanza* is like Isaac Stern sitting in with Lawrence Welk." Ouch! Roberts shuttled through various projects before, disdain intact, starring in the '80s hit *Trapper John M.D.* "I really don't know what the thrust of the series is," he said with customary, paint-peeling candor. "I took the job to financially cover my ass." Roberts regretted none of his choices: "If you're locked into a philosophy of nickels and dimes, then you have pretty limited approach to life."

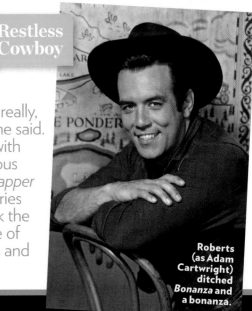
Roberts (as Adam Cartwright) ditched *Bonanza* and a bonanza.

AS A
YOUNG
MAN

"I love to
write,"
Salinger (in
1951) said
in 1974,
"but I write
just for
myself."

Revered
Recluse

J.D.
SALINGER

1919-2010
CORNISH, N.H.

One editor rejected *The Catcher in the Rye* because he couldn't tell whether its alienated hero, Holden Caufield, was meant to be insane. Luckily, Little, Brown saw the light: *Catcher*, a coming-of-age novel for the ages, sold 60 million copies and made its author an icon. Which he hated. America's most famous literary recluse, who died at 91, spent the next 50 years in Cornish, fiercely protecting his privacy with silence, lawsuits and a fence. "He liked privacy, but he was not nasty to people," said a neighbor. Salinger wrote daily, but, said an ex-girlfriend, thought publication too revealing—like, he said, walking "down Madison Avenue with [your] pants down."

the CATCHER
in the RYE

a novel by **J. D. SALINGER**

Alexander HAIG

1924-2010
BALTIMORE

A WARRIOR statesman, Alexander Haig won the Distinguished Service Cross in Vietnam and served as Ronald Reagan's Secretary of State. But it was during the Nixon years that he took on the defining tasks of a long career. As a member of the National Security Council, he helped extricate the U.S. from Vietnam; as Richard Nixon's chief of staff, Haig—in the words of Henry Kissinger—held "our government together as its Presidency disintegrated."

"Wherever he served," Kissinger said of Haig, "he made a difference."

THEY HAD been married nearly 25 years, but on the set of *That Evening Sun* in 2008, Dixie Carter and Hal Holbrook acted like newlyweds. They "were tender and playful," recalled a producer. "It was clear that they were very much in love."

Sadly, their first film together was also their last. On April 10, Carter, 70, passed away due to complications from cancer. A heartbroken Holbrook, 85, said in a statement, "This has been a terrible blow to our family."

Best-known for playing the sassy Julia Sugarbaker in *Designing Women*, the Tennessee native claimed singing as her first love but worked mainly in TV, including *Diff'rent Strokes* and a guest stint on *Desperate Housewives*. "There aren't many people in this town with such class," said *Housewives* creator Marc Cherry. "She will be missed."

Dixie
CARTER

1939-2010
HOUSTON

Lena
HORNE

1917-2010

NEW YORK CITY

I WAS A TEST case for Hollywood," Lena Horne said of the MGM contract she signed in 1942. "And I was a test case for audiences. Would they accept a black woman who wasn't a servant or a native girl or a prostitute type singing a song in an all-white movie? It really seems so silly now."

It didn't then, and much credit for that change belongs to the electrifying actress-singer who, said Halle Berry, broke boundaries "just by breathing. For the first time everyone looked at an African-American woman and really considered her beautiful and powerful. It was empowering."

All-American Mom

Barbara
BILLINGSLEY

1915-2010

SANTA MONICA, CALIF.

The Cleavers were the *Modern Family* of a time when cars had tailfins and everybody liked Ike, and Barbara Billingsley, who played June Cleaver, was the perfectly coiffed, cookie-baking matriarch. Billingsley, who appeared in every episode of *Leave It to Beaver,* which ran from 1957 to 1963, "was as happy as a lark being recognized as America's mom," said Tony Dow, 65, who played older son Wally. Jerry Mathers, 62, a.k.a. "the Beav," called Billingsley "a patient adviser and teacher" who showed him "the importance of manners and respect." Billingsley, who died at 94, was not above a bit of subversive fun: In 1980 she had a hilarious turn as a jive-talking passenger in *Airplane!.* But she will be forever remembered wearing an apron and pearls and saying to Hugh Beaumont, her TV husband, "Ward, I'm worried about the Beaver."

June Cleaver "was the ideal mother," Billingsley said to *TV Guide* in 1997.

Tom BOSLEY

1927-2010
PALM SPRINGS

He won a Tony on Broadway and played a crime-solving priest on TV, but Tom Bosley was born to be Mr. Cunningham, the gruff but tenderhearted father on *Happy Days,* the hit '70s sitcom. For 10 years he sat in an easy chair and doled out sage advice to son Ritchie (Ron Howard) and the Fonz (Henry Winkler), becoming one of television's most beloved dads. Bosley, 83, was so identified with *Happy Days* that his wife once joked that his headstone should read, "Here lies Mr. C., who used to be Mr. B."

"Tom led by example and made us all laugh while he was doing it," said Ron Howard.

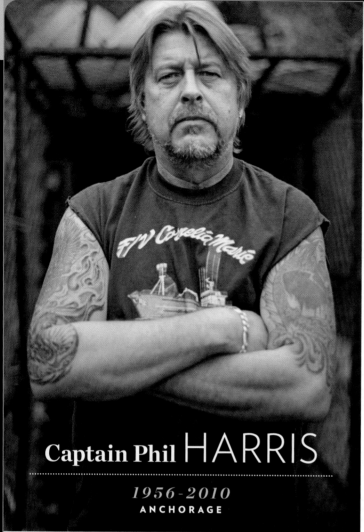

Captain Phil HARRIS

1956 - 2010
ANCHORAGE

Crab
King

T he best way to remember my father," said Josh Harris, "is like Benji, the dog at the pound that's just shaggy and dirty but looks so cute you've just got to take him home." Which is exactly what television viewers did.

Captain Phil Harris was a fan favorite on Discovery's hit reality series *Deadliest Catch,* which chronicled the lives of crab fishermen in the Bering Sea. "To him, it was just a job," said best friend Dan Mittman. "He couldn't believe anybody would sit around and watch crab fishermen!" Harris loved spending up to 10 months a year on his vessel the *Cornelia Marie* and, despite the risks, "tried to have fun every day that he lived," said his other son, Jake, 25, who like Josh, 27, served on the crew.

After suffering a stroke while off-loading crab in Alaska on Jan. 29, Harris held on for 11 days, which gave him time to say goodbye to family and friends. "He was one of the meanest-looking people you'd ever meet," said Josh, "but one of the softest hearts you'd ever find."

Rue McCLANAHAN

Golden
Girl

1934 - 2010
NEW YORK CITY

S he had an earlier role on *Maude,* but for Rue McClanahan the gig of a lifetime was playing the trailblazing cougar Blanche Devereaux on the hit '80s sitcom *The Golden Girls.* "A damn piece of luck," the Healdton, Okla.-born actress said of landing the role, which brought her fame and an Emmy. "I thank the powers that be every day."

It may be been the role she was born to play: A vivacious and outgoing soul, McClanahan married six times and, after her most recent divorce become final in 2009, had fallen for a new beau. "Seven," she told a friend, "is a lucky number!"

McClanahan passed away at 76 of a cerebral hemorrhage. "I will remember the laughs she gave us," said director Del Shores, a pal, "because there were thousands."

ON WITH
THE SHOW

McClanahan was adapting her book *My First Five Husbands...* as a musical when she died.

Corey
HAIM

1971-2010
LOS ANGELES

WHEN you're 15 and there's a Ferrari you just bought and you can't even drive, and all the most beautiful girls in the world—a lot of them older—[are] hitting on [you]," said a friend, "it throws you for a loop."

Sadly, that's a pretty good description of Corey Haim's short life. A teen-throb sensation in movies like *The Lost Boys*, he slipped into addiction and never escaped. Although a coroner determined that drugs did not play a role in the 38-year-old actor's death— blamed on heart and lung problems—an investigation revealed that, by "shopping doctors," he had obtained 553 pills, including Vicodin, the week before he died. By then he was so far from stardom that his family had to auction off some of his belongings to pay for his funeral.

COME
HITHER?

"I got a lot of
girls while I was
at the peak,"
Curtis told
PEOPLE in 2008.
"If I didn't get
them, I got their
stand-ins."

Tony CURTIS

1925-2010
HENDERSON, NEV.

Reflecting on his career in Hollywood, Tony Curtis told PEOPLE, "I was a good-looking kid. That's the only reason I got into the movies." Curtis, who died Sept. 29 at age 85 from cardiac arrest, certainly capitalized on his assets: He appeared in more than 100 films, with roles ranging from a slave in *Spartacus* to a musician in drag in *Some Like It Hot.*

His looks kept him busy offscreen as well. He romanced Marilyn Monroe and Natalie Wood, married five times and had six children (including actress Jamie Lee Curtis with his wife of 11 years, Janet Leigh). Most recently he lived a quieter life in Las Vegas with wife Jill VandenBerg and focused on his other passion, painting.

Through it all, the actor—born Bernard Schwartz, a poor kid from New York City—never lost touch with his pre-fame self. "Although he looked, smelled, dressed, traveled and ate different than his old friends, they knew that somewhere under his glow and fancy cars lurked Bernie Schwartz, and they loved him for it," Jamie Lee told PEOPLE. Indeed, as his widow told mourners at an Oct. 4 memorial, "People always wonder what he was really like. He was exactly like you thought he would be. He was that charming, handsome man you saw on the screen."

GIRL TALK

In Some Like It Hot, Curtis (with Marilyn Monroe) was dressed in drag and on the run from the Mob.

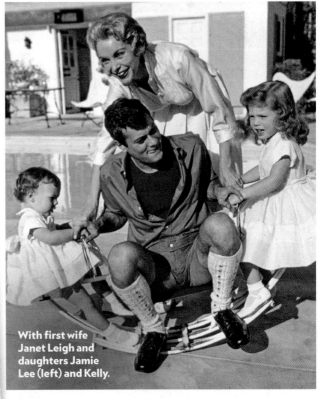

With first wife Janet Leigh and daughters Jamie Lee (left) and Kelly.

EDITOR Cutler Durkee **DESIGN DIRECTOR** Andrea Dunham
ART DIRECTOR Cass Spencer **PHOTO DIRECTOR** Chris Dougherty
PHOTO EDITOR C.Tiffany Lee-Ramos **DESIGNER** Margarita Mayoral
WRITERS Tom Gliatto, Ellen Shapiro, Alex Tresniowski
REPORTER Mary Hart **COPY CHIEF** Ben Harte **SCANNERS** Brien Foy,
Stephen Pabarue **IMAGING** Francis Fitzgerald (Imaging Director),
Rob Roszkowski (Imaging Manager), Romeo Cifelli, Charles Guardino
(Imaging Coordinator Managers), Jeff Ingledue **SPECIAL THANKS TO**
Céline Wojtala, David Barbee, Jane Bealer, Stacie Fenster, Margery
Frohlinger, Ean Sheehy, Patrick Yang

TIME HOME ENTERTAINMENT **PUBLISHER** Richard Fraiman
GENERAL MANAGER Steven Sandonato **EXECUTIVE
DIRECTOR, MARKETING SERVICES** Carol Pittard **DIRECTOR,
RETAIL & SPECIAL SALES** Tom Mifsud **DIRECTOR, NEW
PRODUCT DEVELOPMENT** Peter Harper **DIRECTOR,
BOOKAZINE DEVELOPMENT & MARKETING** Laura Adam
PUBLISHING DIRECTOR, BRAND MARKETING Joy Butts
ASSISTANT GENERAL COUNSEL Helen Wan **BOOK
PRODUCTION MANAGER** Suzanne Janso **DESIGN &
PREPRESS MANAGER** Anne-Michelle Gallero **BRAND
MANAGER** Michela Wilde **ASSISTANT BRAND MANAGER**
Melissa Joy Kong **SPECIAL THANKS TO** Christine Austin, Jeremy
Biloon, Glenn Buonocore, Jim Childs, Susan Chodakiewicz, Rose
Cirrincione, Jacqueline Fitzgerald, Carrie Frazier, Lauren Hall,
Malena Jones, Brynn Joyce, Mona Li, Robert Marasco, Kimberly
Marshall, Amy Migliaccio, Brooke Reger, Dave Rozzelle, Ilene
Schreider, Adriana Tierno, Alex Voznesenskiy, Vanessa Wu

Copyright © 2010 Time Home Entertainment Inc. Published by People Books, an imprint of Time Home Entertainment Inc., 135 West 50th Street, New York, N.Y. 10020. All rights reserved. No part of this book may be reproduced in any form or by any electronic or mechanical means, including information storage and retrieval systems, without permission in writing from the publisher, except by a reviewer, who may quote brief passages in a review. People is a registered trademark of Time Inc. We welcome your comments and suggestions about People Books. Please write to us at People Books, Attention: Book Editors, P.O. Box 11016, Des Moines, IA 50336-1016. If you would like to order any of our hardcover Collectors Edition books, please call us at 1-800-327-6388 (Monday through Friday, 7 a.m.-8 p.m., or Saturday, 7 a.m.-6 p.m. Central Time).

ISBN 10: 1-60320-145-9, ISBN 13: 978-1-60320-145-2, ISSN: 1522-5895

FRONT COVER (clockwise from top right) Photography by Simone & Martin Photography Photographs Copyright © 2010 Willow Tree Productions, LLC; Kyle Rover/Startraks; Robert Kenney/Retna; NBC-Photofest; Nigel Parry/CPi; Storms Media Group; Melanie Dunea/CPi

CONTENTS **2-3** (clockwise from top left) Brian Doben; Photography by Simone & Martin Photography Photographs Copyright © 2010 Willow Tree Productions, LLC; Chip Somodevilla/Getty Images; Gregorio T. Binuya/Everett; Ron Cruz/TLP; Moises Naveira/National Photo Group; Photofest; Disney

NEWS & EVENTS **5** Armando Gallo/Retna; **6** (top) Maciel/X 17; (bottom from left) ©2010, RAZZIEAE Awards, LLC; Monica Almeida/The NY Times/Redux; Vince Bucci/The PictureGroup; Skip Bolen/INF; Deano-Benassi/Splash News; **7** Peter Kramer/AP; **8-9** U.S. Coast Guard/Reuters; (inset) Atlas Press; **10** Nigel Parry/CPi; **11** (from top) Lori Moffett/AP; Chuck Burton/AP; **12-13** (from left) Logan Abassi/UN Photo/Sipa; Ricardo Arduengo/AP; Damon Winter/The New York Times/Redux; **14** Peter Yang/August; (inset) Adam Larkey/ABC; **15** (clockwise from top) Robert Kenney/Retna; Michael Caulfield/Getty Images; Courtesy Playgirl; Amy Sussman/Getty Images; **16** Clive Rose/Getty Images; (inset) Alexander Hassenstein/Bongarts/Getty Images; **17** (clockwise from top left) Roger L. Wollenberg/UPI/Landov; Alex Livesey/Getty Images; Kyodo/Landov; Robyn Beck/AFP/Getty Images; **18** Barcroft/Fame; **19** Courtesy Kevin Smith; **20** (from top) Jean-Paul Aussenard/Wireimage; Damian Dovarganes/AP; Sharky/Splash News; **21** Nigel Parry/CPi; **22** (right, from top) Dave Roback/The Republican/AP; Michael S. Gordon/AP; Christopher Evans/Boston Herald/Polaris; John Suchocki/AP; Christopher Evans/Boston Herald/Polaris; Michael S. Gordon/AP; **23** (clockwise from top left) Courtesy Rolling Stone Magazine; Peter Kramer/AP; James Whatling/Splash News; Dave Allocca/Startraks; **24** (from top) Peter Kramer/NBC Newswire/AP; NY Post/Splash News; News of the World/AP; **25**.

STAR TRACKS **28-29** Justin Stephens/August; **30** Vince Bucci/PictureGroup; **31** (clockwise from top right) Kevin Mazur/Wireimage; Splash News; Jeff Kravitz/Filmmagic; Kevin Mazur/Wireimage; Vince Bucci/PictureGroup; **32** Ramey; (inset) Splash News; **33** (clockwise from left) Mike/Fame; Dean-Pictorica/National Photo Group(3); **34** (clockwise from top) Splash News; Fame; Filmmagic; **35** (clockwise from top right) Richie Buxo/Splash News; Almasi/Bauer-Griffin; Hammond-Millar/Splash News; Rex USA; John Barrett/Globe; **36** Lucas Jackson/Reuters(2); **37** (clockwise from top) PA Photos/Landov; Bauer-Griffin; Lane Ericcson/Photolink

CRIME **38** (clockwise from bottom right) The Oregonian/Landov; Courtesy Multnomah County Sheriff's Office(2); **39** Courtesy Multnomah County Sheriff's Office; **40** (clockwise from bottom right) Entertainment Press/Splash News; Atlas Press; RD-Leon/Retna; Steven Hirsch/Splash News; **41** (clockwise from left) Karel Navarro/AP; Splash News; Atlas Press; AP; **42-43** (clockwise from top left) University of Virginia Media Relations/AP; Andrew Shurtleff/The Daily Progress/AP; The Huntsville Times/Landov; Steve Helber/AP; Charlottesville Police Dept./AP; **44** (clockwise from top left) Santa Monica Police/AP; LA County Sheriff's Dept./AP(3); **45** (bottom) Meredith Griffith/Courtesy Islands Sounder/AP; **46** (clockwise from top left) Matt Stone/Boston Herald/Polaris; Nancy Lane/Boston Herald/AP; Elise Amendola/AP; Courtesy Ben Giles; Courtesy Cory Wynne; **47** (clockwise from top) Courtesy Elaine Aradillas; Damian Dovarganes/AP; Robert Gallagher; X 17

BODY **48** Trae Patton/NBCU Photo Bank; **49** Marc Royce; **50** Courtesy Kate Gosselin; **51** Brian Doben; **52** (clockwise

from top left) Mark Savage/Corbis; John Shearer/Wireimage; Kathy Hutchins/Hutchins; Richard Brill/Startraks; **53** (clockwise from top left) Michael Wright/Wenn; Kevin Winter/Getty Images; Courtesy Jenny Craig/Wenn; Landov; **54-55** Art Streiber/August(2)

MOVIES **56-57** Disney; **58** (from top) Warner Bros.; **59** (clockwise from top) Columbia Tri-Star; Peter Iovino/CBS Films; Barry Wetcher/Columbia Tri-Star; Melissa Moseley/Lionsgate; Andrew Cooper/Disney; Paramount Pictures; Everett

TELEVISION **60** Danny Feld/ABC/Getty Images; **62** (clockwise from left) Chris Cuffaro-Miranda Penn Turin/FOX; Emily Shur/MTV; Daniel-Mauceri/INF; Dana Edelson/NBCU(2); **63** Andrew Eccles/ABC/Getty Images; (insets from left) Mario Perez/ABC/Getty Images; Michael Becker/FOX

MUSIC **64** (clockwise from top left) Jon Furniss/Wireimage; PA Photos/Landov(2); Camera Press/Retna; Ramey; Michael Caulfield/Wireimage; Frank Micelotta/PictureGroup; Jimi Celeste/Patrick McMullan/Sipa; **65** (clockwise from left) Andreas Branch/Patrick McMullan/Sipa; Xposure; Mark Davis/CBS/Landov; Dzilla/Bauer-Griffin; Ibanez/National Photo Group; **66** (clockwise from top right) Ari Michelson/EMI; Vallery Jean/Filmmagic; Storms Media Group; INF; Rex USA; **67** C. Flanigan/Filmmagic; (inset) Splash News

WEDDINGS **68-69** Genevieve de Manio; **70** Genevieve de Manio; **71** (clockwise from top) Genevieve de Manio; Michael Weschler/Corbis Outline; Barbara Kinney; **72-73** Photography by Simone & Martin Photography Photographs Copyright © 2010 Willow Tree Productions, LLC; **74** Kwaku Alston/Corbis Outline; **75** Jason Merritt/Getty Images; **76-77** GSI Media(2); **78-79** (clockwise from left) Mario Anzuoni/Reuters; Pascal Le Segretain/

Getty Images; Jonas Ekstromer/Getty Images; **80** Jeff Kravitz/Wireimage; **81** (from top) Robert Evans/Getty Images; Schneider Press/Sipa; **82** Jonathan Friolo/National Photo Group; **83** Anthony Vazquez/Courtesy Kevin and Danielle Jonas; **84** Stephanie Pistel; **85** (from top) Kevin Winter/Getty Images; Lucien Capehart/Getty Images; **86-87** Jesus Carrero/Hola!(3)

ENGAGEMENTS **88** Danny Moloshok/Reuters; **89** (clockwise from top) Vince Flores/AFF; Stephen Danelian; Eric Charbonneau/Wireimage; Byron Purvis/Admedia; **90** Amedeo M. Turello/Palais Princier Monaco/Getty Images; **91** (from top) Rick Diamond/Getty Images; Steve Granitz/Wireimage

BABIES **92-93** Omar Cruz; **94** Joe Pugliese; **95** Joe Buissink; **96** Alison Dyer; **97** Albert Michael/Startraks; **98** Thornton-Dario/INF; **99** Brian Doben

SPLITS **101** Jeff Kravitz/Filmmagic; **102** John Shearer/Wireimage; **103** (from top) John Shearer/Wireimage; Jen Lowery/Startraks; **104** Brian To/Elevation/PictureGroup; **105** John Shearer/Wireimage; **106** (from top) Kevin Mazur/Wireimage; Rose Billings/Landov; **107** Evan Agostini/AP; **108** Kwaku Alston/Corbis Outline; **109** (clockwise from top) Jamie Trueblood/Disney Channel; GSI Media; Evan Agostini/Getty Images; **110** (from top) Francois Ferrand; Stephen d'Antal/Rex USA; **111** Marc Royce

FASHION **112** Juan Soliz/Pacific Coast News; **114** (from left) Tsuni/Gamma; Jason Merritt/Getty Images; INF; Benkey/AFF; **115** (from left) Tsuni/Gamma; Maria Ramirez/FWD; Brad Weingarden/PictureGroup; **116** (from left) Jason Merritt/Getty Images; Chris Canada/Retna; Kevin Winter/Getty Images; BEImages; **117** (from left) Vince Flores/Celebrity Photo; Quasar/Star Max; Jason Merritt/Getty Images; **118** (from left) Axelle/Bauer-Griffin; Jon Kopaloff/Filmmagic; Los

Angeles Daily News/Zuma; Chris Pizzello/AP; **119** (from left) Mark J. Terrill/AP; Jason Merritt/Getty Images; Kyle Rover/Startraks; **120** (from left) DP/AAD/Star Max; INF; Jason Merritt/Getty Images; Kyle Rover/Startraks; **121** (from left) Jim E. Safire/Loud & Clear; RD-Kirkland/Retna; Lionel Hahn/Abaca; **122** (from left) Rex USA; SPW/Splash News; Tony DiMaio/iPhoto; Jon Leibson/Splash News; **123** (from left) Adam Orchon/Elevation/PictureGroup; Jason LaVeris/Filmmagic; Marc Malabar/Most Wanted

TRIBUTES **124-125** Dick Zimmerman/Shooting Star; (inset) NBCU Photo Bank; **126** (from top) Michael Halsband/Landov; Reuters; **127** Eyevine/Zuma; **128** Bryce Duffy/Corbis; **129** Andreas Branch/Patrick McMullan/Sipa; **130** Everett/NBCU; **131** (from top) Bob D'Amico/ABC Photo Archives/Getty Images; MPTV; **132** Bruce McBroom/MPTV; **133** Michael Childers/Sygma/Corbis; **134** Michael Ochs Archives/Getty Images; **135** (from top) Wenn; Bud Gray/MPTV; Bettmann/Corbis; **136** (from top) Evening Standard/Getty Images; Little, Brown & Company/AP; Mark Reinstein/IPOL/Globe; **137** Steve Schapiro/Corbis; **138** Virgil Apger/Kobal; **139** (from top) Gabi Rona/MPTV; Charles William Bush/MPTV; ABC Photo Archives/Getty Images; **140** (from top) Blair Bunting/Discovery Channel/Getty Images; Theo Westenberger/NBCU Photo Bank; **141** Dino May/Shooting Star; **142** Photofest; **143** (from left) Neal Peters Collection; Globe

BACK COVER (clockwise from top left) Chris Graythen/Getty Images; Jason Kempin/Wireimage; Santa Monica Police Dept./AP; Rupert Hartley/Rex USA; Miranda Penn Turin/FOX; EMI Music; U.S. Coast Guard/Reuters; Disney; Kevin Perkins/Pacific Coast News; Steve Granitz/Wireimage